HAS THE CHURCH A FUTURE?

HAS THE CHURCH
A FUTURE?

by
Douglas John Hall

THE WESTMINSTER PRESS
Philadelphia

Scripture quotations, unless otherwise specified, are
from the Revised Standard Version of the Bible copy-
righted 1946, 1952, © 1971, 1973 by the Division of
Christian Education of the National Council of the
Churches of Christ in the U.S.A., and are used by
permission.

BOOK DESIGN BY DOROTHY ALDEN SMITH

First edition

Published by The Westminster Press®
Philadelphia, Pennsylvania

PRINTED IN THE UNITED STATES OF AMERICA

9 8 7 6 5 4 3 2 1

Library of Congress Cataloging in Publication Data

Hall, Douglas John, 1928–
Has the church a future?

1. Church. 2. Mission of the church.
3. Christianity—20th century. I. Title.
BV600.2.H25   262'.7   79–29647
ISBN 0-664-24308-8

To my first teachers—

Irene Sandick Hall

John Darius Hall
(1907–1953)

CONTENTS

continued

continued

When He created man, God gave him a secret—and that secret was not how to begin but how to begin again.

. . . It is not given to man to begin; that privilege is God's alone. But it is given to man to begin again—and he does so every time he chooses to defy death and side with the living.

Elie Wiesel

PREFACE

In 1967 my country celebrated its hundredth birthday. Getting into the spirit of the occasion, a denominational publication took on the assignment of predicting what the church in Canada would look like in a hundred years. Here is a sample of their brief scenario:

In 2067, over 90 per cent of Canadians will tell the census-taker they are Christian. . . .

Ministers will complain that the majority give meagre support, attend irregularly—mostly at Christmas and Easter—and call on them for marrying and cremating purposes. . . .

Young people will complain that old men dominate the discussions in church councils.

Women will complain that men dominate the discussions in church councils.

Laymen will say that the clergy dominate everything. . . .

Karl Barth will be considered the only important theologian of the 20th century.

All ministers will be given intensive training in psychology.

Most churches will have a large paid staff of lay-men.

The basic salary for ministers will be $28,000 a year. The average pension will be $31,000. . . .

The Bishop of Uranium City will be on the carpet for saying he didn't believe in the virgin birth, the physical resurrection, apostolic succession, or infant baptism. . . .

The "God-Is-Dead" school of theology of the mid-20th century will not have been heard of for 97 years.

Centennial speakers will discover that 100 years ago some Christians actually defended capital punishment, in the 18th century Christians engaged in the slave trade, in the 19th they defended war, in the 20th they discriminated against Negroes, and in the 21st the rich exploited the poor, and the powerful oppressed the weak.

A careful study of these "Predictions" could tell us much about the mentality of a significant cross section of our society and its churches. I cite them here for the more limited purpose of introducing, in a concrete way, two particular assumptions I intend to challenge in this book. The first assumption is that Christianity is, and will continue to be, the majority religion of the Western world—and perhaps of the world at large. The second assumption is that this is as it should be.

I do not know what statistical research informed the "Predictions," but it would appear quite one-sided, to say the least. One piece of information alone throws the whole scenario into some disorder: In the same denomination responsible for this publication, the average age of church members today is fifty (in Montreal, I am told, it is sixty-five). The average age of people in the country at large is thirty-five. Similar data could be produced in considerable abundance. But it is unprofitable to carry on the discussion at that level. Statistics, as well as sociological data of many sorts, are, to be sure, significant in theological reflection. But by themselves they cannot dislodge fixed beliefs. And what informs the "Predictions" is fixed beliefs. They issue from an ecclesiastical-theological frame of mind that is simply not open to the prospect that the real posture of the church in the contemporary world may be that of a minority in a pluralistic civilization. This mentality is so deeply committed to the idea of "church as majority" that it can entertain only data which confirm that model.

The "church as majority" (Constantinian) concept of Christianity is an extremely powerful and entrenched model, one by which we are *all* deeply conditioned. It functions, in fact, as an ideology, and, like all ideologies, it eliminates in advance everything in actual experience that would seriously call it in question.

Ideologies are never partial; they embrace the universe. Thus it is not surprising that in the process of omitting all negating evidence from its vision of the church of 2067 as a triumphant (if rather lukewarm) majority, the "Predictions" eliminate the radical negative from their implicit account of the world at large. One looks in vain in the "Predictions" for any hint of the "future shock" which has become so indigenous to our epoch that even the most smug elements of our society cannot wholly escape it.

I am reflecting on this statement in particular because it is typical of a whole important segment of our "First World." It is all too typical that the "Predictions" can speak about the future without reference to the great physical crises by which our whole planet is beset: famine, war, poverty, depletion of vital resources, rampant pollution and devastation of nature, overpopulation, etc. It fits the type, too, when it passes over the even more staggering spiritual problems of the race: the technological reduction of humanity to the mass; the disappearance of spontaneity and dignity; the loss of a sense of purpose in existing. Even to assume that there will be an entity called "Canada" a hundred years from now is to indulge either in a great act of political faith or in extreme rashness!

In the "Predictions," and the type of thought they represent, we have subtle reinforcement of the status quo. This kind of utterance assures people that the Christian and human situation in the future will be about the same as they believe it is today. Women will have made a little—but not excessive!—headway in their attempt to achieve the full status of human persons. The oppressed of the world are still held under by the rich. The ecclesiastical structures will have been altered only slightly, with ecumenical lines drawn up just a little differently. There will still be sufficient monies in the churches to pay relatively large salaries to clergy, and even larger pensions to retired clergy—and to employ hordes of lay persons as well. The great issues of theology will be those of the virgin birth, the physical resurrection, apostolic succession, and infant baptism. God will be so thoroughly present that no one will be moved to recall those who once feared he had "died" (is the psalmist also included here?).

The importance of such statements does not lie in their details but in their general character. The "Predictions" demonstrate graphically the manner in which this type of thinking *about the church* is regularly accompanied by an acceptance and promotion of the *status quo of the society.* It is a "package deal." The same mentality that needs to have the religious establishment preserved intact requires that the society in which that religion functions should also be preserved intact. There are parallels in the business world. No manufacturer is interested exclusively in selling a product. In order to ensure a market for a product called "Future Wax," Johnston's has at the same time to "sell" the ultramodern society that finds such a product attractive. Similarly, a religious institution that operates on the assumptions of cultic religion is never content with the promotion of its own message. It must uphold as well the culture that seems to want it. It must make itself appealing to that culture and live within the boundaries of that culture's values, expectations, and taboos.

Therefore, while this mentality is able to open itself to surface criticism and change, it will not allow itself to dwell upon *any* problems, whether religious or secular, that may demand radical analysis and transformation. The question raised in the title of this book is simply not permitted to invade the consciousness of those who cultivate the "Christian majority" mentality. To wonder whether *the church* has a future is, to such a mind-set, to wonder whether the whole social fabric of which the church is part has a future. In the presence of such questions, representatives of this type of thinking respond with scorn or humor—as if it were ludicrous to find anyone seriously asking such things!

Iconoclastic critics of the churches are apt to dismiss this mentality. I cannot do so, because I find it a powerful force in the churches, especially the so-called "major denominations," and more particularly among the clergy. Being found within both of these categories myself, I have an inherent sympathy for those who exemplify this state of mind. It is not easy to hear questions like "Has the church a future?" when what is bound up with the continuation and growth of Christendom is not only one's ecclesiastical and societal preferences but one's personal security as well. It *is* comforting, on the other hand, to learn that way on into the future there will still be comfortable stipends, pensions, and amenities, as well as the usual dignities attaching to the office of ministry. It is equally consoling for worried people in today's congregations to hear that the greatest problems they will likely face in the future are just extensions of the difficulties that occupy them now.

While I have sympathy for the very human origins of this mentality, I have to speak up against it. It is just this mentality, this false and unwarranted complacency, that is preventing the church of Jesus Christ from getting on with its real work in the world today. There is a vital role awaiting a church that is ready to face, honestly, its minority status in the world. It could become a prophetic witness to truth in an age of deceit, a friend of the oppressed, a cartographer of the peculiar night into which Western civilization has been sinking for generations, a searcher for the Light that shines in darkness. But because we want to continue thinking of ourselves in the kind of terms laid down—openly and covertly—in the "Predictions"; because we want to be the church that is "like a mighty army," we are missing the opportunities for real ministry that open out today to Christ's "little flocks."

This study is not written *against* the majority mentality, damaging as it is; it is written *for* another group of Christians in the churches and on their periphery. I mean the growing numbers of those who *do* sense the death of Christendom and who are asking whether the church (and our society!) has a future. It would be surprising indeed if nothing of that kind of questioning were to be found in the churches. For the "humiliation of Christendom" is not something peculiar to the last few decades; it has been going on for several centuries. Its origins can be traced to the breakdown of the Middle Ages and the beginnings of the Renaissance. By the eighteenth century there were already quite definite alternatives to the church for large numbers of people. Recent "serial history," based on wills and other legal documents, shows a marked shift of the general populace of Europe away from the church. Analyzing twenty thousand eighteenth-century wills from Provence, Michel Vovelle (*Piété baroque et déchristianisation en Provence au xviiie siècle;* Paris: Plon, 1973) records that

> One conclusion is inescapable: "dechristianisation" was well on its way before the French Revolution. Pious formulas and money spent on masses takes a sharp downward turn around 1760. No great "event" is recorded for that period in our Church histories. But the mind of the authors of the wills is massively shifting. (Michel Despland, "Comparative Religious Ethics: Early Modern European Problems"; Concordia University, Montreal; unpublished paper, 1978)

There are still pockets in the modern world where it can seem that the church is in a position of great promi-

nence and influence. Not all of them are backwaters of
civilization. Particularly in the United States, whose history has been filled with religious "renewals" of one
kind and another, today yet another wave of religious
activity can be noticed. It sometimes appears that the
world is indeed being "conquered for Christ." But we
must not be misled by regional trends or by thinking
that moves in decades. Nor should we assume that everything that goes on under the name "Christian" has
any genuine connection with the historic faith. The reduction of Christendom that this book assumes has a
long history. While periodic and geographic fluctua-
tions can certainly be noted, it cannot be doubted that
the general trend is toward minority status for Christians in the world. The question is not whether we approve of this, or should try to stop it. The question is
whether we as Christians shall have the grace and insight to adjust our concept of the church to this sociological reality—and to do so *in hope.*

This leads to the second assumption in the "Predictions" that I intend to challenge. It is far more subtle
and infinitely more dangerous than the first. For the
first only indulges rather innocently in the idea that
Christianity is and will continue to be the majority religion that it has been for centuries. The second assumption is the belief that precisely this is what the church
should be.

The latter assumption is the foundational one, the
psychological explanation behind the selective myopia
of the first. The conviction that Christianity *should be*
the dominant if not exclusive religion of humankind
requires the historical and sociological insistence that
that is precisely what it *is* and *will be.*

So profoundly established is the image of the church as majority that in every situation known to me in North America where the real *minority* status of Christianity has become conspicuous, those involved are tempted to a debilitating melancholy. What prevents them more than anything else from being the church *as* and *where* they are is their feeling of having failed. Looming large before them is the sixteen-centuries-old image of the church as majority. It is embodied for them in their buildings, hymns, and liturgies. On account of it, they have a built-in distrust of every attempt to legitimize themselves as a minority. Such attempts are suspect even when they emanate from their own imagination and discourse, their Bible study, and whatever inspiration they may have, now and then, from studies such as the present one. The specter of the "successful" congregation hangs over their head like the sword of Damocles. Often it takes the shape of their own "successful" past. And there are always a few apparently successful congregations in the vicinity which help to confirm for them the miserable fact that they have failed.

I have written this book for these failures especially. I am tempted to add that it is written *against* all "successful" congregations and other Christian enterprises, except that lately I have found in some of these apparently thriving places an astonishing openness to precisely the analysis I have made here. Even in the American Bible Belt I discovered a significant minority that could receive this interpretation of Christian existence today as true. There are few groups of Christians on the scene today who can still pretend to *great* success. But at a deeper level there are some, even in the most triumphalistic ecclesiastical situations, who are disturbed by the smell of success. They find something missing in the midst of all that shouting. In a world that is not eminently "successful" itself, a successful church can have something of the same reputation as successful multinational corporations!

I believe there is beginning to be an openness throughout old Christendom today to another way of being the church. When Søren Kierkegaard launched his scathing "attack upon Christendom" more than a hundred years ago, he was made the brunt of cruel cartoons. Perhaps he died of ridicule. There are still many in the churches who cannot bear to have Christendom attacked. But there are others by now among the rank and file of Christians who have begun to suspect that Kierkegaard had something. It was something which did not originate with him, but which can be traced like a thin antiphonal response throughout all the ages of the church: a different tune from the one that was sung by the majority, but all the same a tune that had to be heard. I would estimate that for every fifty church members who want to shut their ears to the judgment (crisis) that is beginning with the household of God there is one who ponders it in his or her heart. I am writing for that one.

For that one let me answer right away the question I have raised in my title: Yes, the church does have a future. I believe that sincerely. But I am equally convinced that it is not, and ought not to be, the future that during most of its history the church has longed and struggled for. It is not the future of the institution that began, under Constantine, to subdue and conquer the whole world. It is not the organization that rejoices at the prospect of 90 percent of my fellow Canadians announcing themselves as "Christians" to the census takers in 2067. Against that institution the gates of hell (and heaven!) are already prevailing. What will withstand the tests of time is something very different.

D.J.H.

Montreal, Quebec

ACKNOWLEDGMENTS

Perhaps there are books that are the creations of their authors alone. This is not one of them. In any case it would be difficult in the field of Christian theology to produce something all by oneself. For theology is a corporate undertaking—the ongoing dialogue of the "body of Christ" as it encounters the ever-changing world.

Like the other books and essays I have written, therefore, this book is a consequence of conversations with Christians and others on this continent and in Europe. It began with a sermon in my home congregation. There were naturally responses, reactions, questions. They led to revision on my part—expansion of the original ideas, further reflection and research, rewriting. It next appeared as a series of lectures presented in Seattle, Washington, under the auspices of the First United Methodist Church. Again there were discussions—agreements, disagreements, enthusiastic support, astonished rejection—provoking further changes.

So the wonder grew! It was offered in various shapes and sizes to groups of lay persons and ministers in Toronto, Chicago, South Carolina, Georgia, and elsewhere. All these people contributed something to the final product, and I am indebted to them. I am indebted also to my students and colleagues at the Faculty of Religious Studies in McGill University, my daily "community of dialogue"; and to my wife and children, who are at the same time the partners and the victims of my physical and spiritual wanderings!

Not that I hold any of these persons responsible for what I have said here. A book of theology cannot be the product of one mind, but neither can it be an assemblage of the ideas of many minds. "Theology by consensus" is one of the great horrors of the modern world! For better or worse, theological thought (and perhaps all thought) can achieve a kind of cohesiveness only as it passes through the sieve of a single life. But the test of its authenticity will be whether it communicates with other lives. I offer this work in the hope that it will do so—especially that it will speak to and for those who regard the future of the church with a certain foreboding, though they have not given up hope.

The book is dedicated to the two people who first taught me to think critically—who introduced me to the magic combination of skepticism and expectancy that is the stuff out of which new beginnings are made.

I

BEGINNING AT THE END

The Death of Christendom

For a decade, my family and I lived on the Canadian prairies, in the beautiful city of Saskatoon on the broad South Saskatchewan River. Often on Sundays we would drive out into the prairies in the ancient car we had then. Some of my students regarded this as an act of faith comparable to that of Abraham, who went out not knowing whither he was going—or whether he would ever return!

On one such Sunday drive, we came across an old church building in an uninhabited region near the river. It stood there against the darkened autumn sky like a pale sentinel of the past. Once it had been painted white. Someone long ago had wired shut the front door, but the back door was open and flapping in the wind. Nothing remained inside the church but the altar and most of the pulpit. There were no pews. Remnants of a pump organ stood in an anteroom. In the basement I found coal in the bin, and firewood that had been there, I suppose, since the church was vacated, presumably just after World War II. And there were dead pigeons—the dust-dry, feathery remains of birds that were once beautiful in flight.

The scene filled me with sadness. I knew it was not an unusual scene. All over the prairies today one can find such nostalgic and melancholy buildings: deserted churches, some simple, some elaborate, once the pride of their communities. And not only in the prairies! In the towns and cities of this continent—those glittering places to which the sons and daughters of our pioneer ancestors flocked for what they dreamed would mean a better chance at life: there, too, are empty churches and churches that will soon be empty. In the great industrial cities of Europe, in which the decline of Christendom is even farther advanced, there are still greater empty churches. In some parts of the world no pretense is made of considering them churches any longer. Tourists are shown buildings that are, architecturally, churches; but the guides speak of them without batting an eyelash as "museums."

So the scene on the prairie that day was for me the symbol of a dying institution, and it filled me with sadness.

The Sense of Abandonment

Even if I had not looked upon that scene as one who professes faith in Jesus as the Christ, I should have been sad. Many of my most sensitive secular acquaintances would have been able to share my melancholy. The life which has replaced that symbolized by these old church buildings—endless television, winters in Hawaii, sprawling concrete cities, and Disneyland—can be thought an improvement over the old world of white village churches only by the vulgar. Indeed, many of the most sensitive people I know are trying desperately to get *back* to the world of the little white churches. They want to discover a life they vaguely remember, or have heard rumors of. It is a life that is real, that avoids the plastic superficiality of the modern age of instant rice and human alienation. Thus being moved to melancholy by a symbol of the death of that former, simpler world of the little white churches is something many people experience. They may have no particular interest in religion, and perhaps no obvious remnants of the ancestral faith left in them.

On believing Christians such scenes can have an especially disquieting effect. In the midst of all that emptiness—not just empty pews but no pews at all; doors wired shut; dead pigeons in the basement!—how can one *believe?* How can one maintain faith, hope, love of the neighbor? How can one hear, as if it were true, the confident statement of the writer of Hebrews:

> Therefore, since we are surrounded by so great a cloud of witnesses, let us also lay aside every weight, and sin which clings so closely, and let us run with perseverance the race that is set before us. (Heb. 12:1)

Surrounded by witnesses? What witnesses? The wind? The dead pigeons? The tombstones in the adjoining graveyard? How can one feel that one is part of a great company, a stirring movement, "the church militant here on earth," when everywhere in once-proud Christendom what one is most conscious of in the churches is empty space? "Like a mighty army moves the church of God," wrote Sabine Baring-Gould a century ago. Where is this army today?

False Alternatives

There are, of course, ways of dealing with this experience—dealing with it in order not to have to deal with it, if you know what I mean. One of them is the way of repression. You close your eyes to the emptiness. You overlook the fact that sanctuaries built to house a thousand seem well attended if there are two hundred worshipers in them of a Sunday. You talk knowingly about urban shift and tell yourself that churches "elsewhere" really are full. In short, you determine to be optimistic. There is a peculiar kind of optimism characteristic of the North American mentality: it grits its teeth and vows to think positively. It blots from consciousness whatever negative things threaten to get in the way. "Official optimism" I call it, because it isn't real.

In that direction lies the greatest folly. One can only cope temporarily by repressing the truth. Sooner or later the truth catches up with us.

Another response to the decimation of Christendom is to try to make Christendom happen all over again. The older, long-established denominations have for the most part given up on that procedure. Heaven knows they've tried to hold on, to keep the power and influence of Christendom from waning, to keep everybody in church. But experience has taught them that it doesn't work. Now the technique of re-creating Christendom seems to have fallen to the former fringe groups, the ultraconservatives and (as they like to style themselves) "the evangelicals." They want to turn the United States and if possible the whole world into the Kingdom of Christ, and they want to do it right now!

They are able to quote impressive statistics—if you are impressed by that sort of thing.

I am not. And I am glad that on the whole my church is not, either. This attempt to revive dying Christendom is not only innocent about the nature of the times in which we live; it is also potentially dangerous. It has not recognized the pretensions of Christian imperialism. It would repeat the crusading triumphalism of the past, as if there were no questions to be asked about that spirit. After Auschwitz and Hiroshima, no form of Christianity has the right to engage in high-pressure tactics to persuade people to become Christians. From now on we shall have to live in a pluralistic world, where Christianity is one way among others. Attempting to fill up the churches that have become empty or partly empty does not solve the problem of the demise of Christendom. Moreover, to act as though the great skeptical and agnostic questions of today had never been raised, or could easily be refuted, is ridiculous. We can't turn back the clock. Neither can we pretend that a fully Christianized world would be a good world. That has already been tried.

Beginning Where We Are

The alternative is to begin where we are: in our empty, or nearly empty, or by no means full churches. For all the worldly melancholy that it may conjure up in us when we recall the supposedly glorious past, this is where we have to begin.

Concretely it means developing the habit of honesty in assessing the Christian situation. We have to learn to be honest about ourselves—qualitatively, quantitatively. Over the last few decades in particular, church people have been indulging in a good deal of statistical exaggeration. It is part of our attempt to repress what we know about the humiliation of Christendom. It has become habitual. We shall have to unlearn repression and learn honesty.

Again, beginning where we are means recognizing that we represent one alternative among others. Not everybody will choose our alternative. Not everybody will want to be baptized, married, and buried by us! Not even those who are born into more-or-less Christian homes. Not even, necessarily, our own sons and daughters. There are many alternatives to the Christian way in today's pluralistic society, and the future will bring increasing freedom to choose those other ways.

Beginning where we are means, in short, recognizing our new status in the world, especially the formerly "Christian" world of the Western Hemisphere. We are a minority. We are few. According to some recent statistics, 33 percent of the world's population is "Christian." This is the kind of statistic we must learn to distrust, because it gives an entirely wrong impression. How many of this 33 percent can even say what the term "Christian" means?

Christendom as Western Christianity imagined it and tried to create it for some sixteen centuries has come to an end. The church as a "mighty army" is no more, and no manner of Christian revivalism can put Humpty Dumpty together again.

It is sobering, even frightening, when Christians in our generation realize this about themselves. It means we are on our own in a way that our grandparents and great-grandparents in the faith never were. They stood in their white prairie churches, and everything seemed to be in place—though, ironically, for countless thousands of their contemporaries in Europe and elsewhere the end of *that* type of Christianity had already come. We are the first generations in this "New World" to realize the end of Christendom. That is probably why so many of us still try to put it off a little longer. Few want to be pioneers in a new, unreceptive, and "strange" land. Few are ready to improvise.

Theodore Roszak said about the youth culture of the late 1960's: "They are improvising their own idea of maturity" (*The Making of a Counter Culture: Reflections on the Technocratic Society and Its Youthful Opposition,* p. 33; Doubleday & Co., Anchor Books, 1969). They have to, he explained, because what they learned about adult life from their parents has been shown up to them as gross immaturity.

So with honest Christians today. Consciously accepting our emptiness and littleness, we have to become improvisers. We can get little help from our immediate predecessors of the little white churches. Many of us find that unnerving. Naturally! We know that many of the things that we try will prove wrong and foolish, just as happened with the adolescents of the counter culture who were improvising their adulthood. Many of our experiments in social action, in worship, in community, in ministry, have already proven unrealistic or inept. This, too, is part of beginning where we are.

Proximity to Our Origins

There is at least one significant advantage that we have over most of our predecessors in Christian faith:

we are closer to the Christian *origins* than almost all of them! Though far away in time, we are close to the earliest Christians in the circumstances of our existence. Contrary to the general impression that has been created by historical Christianity, the church of the New Testament was not a "mighty army" either. Like us, it was a scattering of "little flocks" here and there. When the writer of Hebrews admonished his readers to have courage because, after all, "we are surrounded by so great a cloud of witnesses," he was writing for small, powerless, poor, and dispersed groups of people—a minority that was hardly even significant enough to deserve the name "minority."

But then, those earliest Christians to whom he wrote would never have thought that what he said about the great cloud of surrounding witnesses had anything to do with church rolls and budgets, and social influence. What spurred them on and gave them hope was not their own power—the power of numbers, of money, of property—but the power of the gospel. It was a message that caused men and women to go out without knowing their destination, to suffer rejection and abuse, to bear witness to truth whatever the consequences.

Therefore, beginning where we are, we are in an excellent position to learn again from our sources, the Scriptures. More than any of those Christians of the past sixteen or so centuries, we can hear the *Biblical* description of "the people of God." As Christians we share with the first Christians a basic similarity: our littleness. Even the Reformers of the sixteenth century, who tried to hear the Bible in a new and fresh way, were still part of a society in which Christianity had become something fundamentally different from the Biblical picture of the church. When the *sociological* circumstances of the church today are altogether different from those at its origin, it is hard to learn *theological* truths from the New Testament, no matter how willing one may be. Our great advantage today, if we will accept it and not try to hide it from ourselves, is that we are close enough to the social situation of the church in the New Testament to be able to hear, afresh, what the New Testament is really saying about the church of Jesus Christ.

The Witnesses There Are

If we listen carefully to that Biblical testimony, without the biases we have acquired on account of Christendom's self-image of grandeur and power in the world, we will discover that we are indeed surrounded by a great cloud of witnesses. In the emptiness we can discover them. In the ruins of once-proud Christendom they can still be heard. Sometimes they speak almost directly out of the past: the letters of Paul, for instance, to those little *koinōnia* groupings in the Mediterranean cities of old, could be heard by us today as if they were meant almost explicitly for us.

But the witnesses are not only voices from the past. Sometimes they appear to us in strange places and with strange identities—angels whom we encounter unawares. Often they are those very nonreligious men and women with whom we brush shoulders every day. Significant numbers of them are groping for something to cling to in this age of uncertainty. They seek something greater than the gratification of their own desires in this "me first" generation. Some of them are angry and afraid over war, deceit, and injustice in the world. Some are mourning the loss of God and meaning. Some (as in *Alice's Restaurant*) even buy up the old, discarded churches, the pews, the pump organs, the bric-a-brac, in something like a poignant effort to keep the Alternative from disappearing forever. (I have developed the thoughts contained in this paragraph more fully in my book *The Reality of the Gospel and the Unreality of the Churches;* Westminster Press, 1975.)

We are not alone, then, after all. There *is* a cloud of witnesses, and perhaps it is much greater than we can possibly imagine. But to perceive even the edges of it, we church folk have to acquire new vision. It has little to do with the explicitly religious assumptions we have traditionally associated with this statement from Hebrews.

The Alpha in the Omega

Two decades ago, a great East German theologian said that we are living today in "the last days of the Constantinian era." (This statement is attributed to Pastor Günther Jacob of Cottbus, and is alluded to by Karl Barth in his *How to Serve God in a Marxist Land,* p. 64; Association Press, 1959.) The church as we have known it, the church that tried to be a "mighty army," the church also of the little wooden buildings and the big brick and stone edifices—in short, "Christendom"—has come to an end.

But if we are alive to the New Testament and the surrounding "witnesses," this end might be the beginning of something more nearly the church of Jesus Christ than anything this world has known until now.

The end of Christendom might be the beginning of the church!

II

REASSESSING OUR PAST

Where Have We Come From?

There comes a time in the lives of most thoughtful persons when they ask about their own past. In a new and sometimes unsettling way, they inquire about the image of themselves they have derived from that past. Where have I come from? What is this road along which I have traveled from my cradle? How did I happen to make that particular turn? Why did I become what I have become? Why a lawyer and not a musician? Why a teacher and not the farmer I once dreamed of becoming? Am I in fact who I seem to be? Am I the same one who started out, long ago, in that little town, the child of those parents, the playmate of those friends? Am I the one that my mate married? Or have I been changed along the way, perhaps radically? Have I become something different now? How should I think about my past, my history? What, precisely, *is* my story?

It is said that this kind of reassessment of ourselves often occurs at the onset of middle age. Perhaps it is middle age! Having recently entered that stage of life myself, I am inclined to think that it is. It can be a devastating experience. Having carried about in one's

38

head a rather well defined picture of oneself, one finds all of a sudden that a very different interpretation is possible—perhaps even necessary. Perhaps the old, comfortable self-image, begun by one's parents and contributed to by one's peers and the whole society, must be exchanged for a new image with which one may be far less comfortable. The story that one has been told, and has in turn told to oneself and others, may have to be retold in another way altogether. In the light of new facts, new prospects, new horizons, one's history is not, after all, something fixed and unchangeable. It isn't just data, information, facts. It is the interpretation of these facts, too. And interpretation can change drastically, depending on one's perspective.

The same thing is true of institutions. Moments come when those involved in an institution feel the need to rethink their purpose, to reexamine the goals that have been envisaged by past generations and the values that they tried to preserve. This can be said even of nations. In fact, every perceptive observer of life on this continent knows that just such a reassessment is called for at this time, and here and there it is occurring. We, the peoples of North America, have been telling a certain story about ourselves for a long time—in fact, from the beginning. We learned this story originally from the great European thinkers of the Renaissance and the Enlightenment. They envisaged a new society, where reason and justice, equality and peace would prevail. America was the place where this new society would take shape: the "New World" for the "new Adam." But certain events in our own recent history (Vietnam, the ecological crises, the depletion of world resources, our apparent complicity in the oppression of the Third

World) have caused us to wonder whether this story that we have been told, and have been telling about ourselves is true. We feel the need to reassess our past. Without that reassessment, we can't account for much that has come to be in these last decades, or that seems likely to occur in the near future.

It almost always happens that this need to reassess the *past* is sparked by a certain apprehensiveness about the *future*. It is hardly surprising that in individual life such a reassessment is associated with "the middle-age crisis." Surely middle age means confronting at the emotional level what one may have known intellectually from the beginning: that one's future is *limited*. We ask, "Where have I come from?" because we realize something of the circumscribed nature of our future. So it is with us as North Americans. No longer so sure that we have an unlimited future, with everything getting "better and better," we know that we have to reassess our past. The cornerstone of our particular past was precisely the assumption that everything would get better and better continually.

A similar experience has come now to the Christian church. As Christians, we have been telling a certain story about ourselves and to ourselves. But in these days that story doesn't square with the facts. Neither does it account for what the keenest observers among us can see for the church on the immediate horizon. We are called by the historical moment in which we find ourselves to reassess our past—to rethink our history in the light of present realities and future prospects. How can we face this challenge?

A Success Story

To begin with, we will only meet the challenge of our historical moment if we are ready to become quite rigorously self-critical—especially in regard to the way we have thought about ourselves heretofore. What *is* the story we Christians have been telling ourselves and others?

It is a story with many versions. Different Christian groupings tell the story differently. Still, a common theme has been running through the length and breadth of these many variations. The common theme that unites them all (perhaps, ironically, the greatest ecumenical commonplace!) is the theme of success. We tell our Christian story as a success story.

That is how you see it presented, implicitly and explicitly, in most of our Christian history texts. Success is the theme celebrated in most of our hymns about the church, in our prayers, in our public pronouncements. This motif, often in its crassest forms, is the great theme of all our denominational variations. The founders or heroes of our particular branch of Christendom come off in the telling as the final champions in the long march toward success: John Knox confronting Mary, Queen of Scots; Luther at the bonfire outside Wittenberg burning the papal bull; Francis Xavier bringing a triumphant Christian faith to the benighted Japanese; John Wesley converting the masses of deprived and depraved workers in newly industrialized England. At last the truth triumphs! At last the enemies are routed! At last the doubters and sinners are won over!

From where we sit in time, the greatest episode in

the Christian success story occurred near the beginning. It was when Christianity was adopted as the official religion of the great Roman Empire. The emperor Constantine the Great won a strategic battle against his enemies under the sign of the cross of Christ (*in hoc signo vinces,* "In this sign conquer": the words Constantine is supposed to have heard in his dream before the battle of the Milvian Bridge, A.D. 312). He subsequently decreed that all the empire should honor this formerly persecuted and illegal religion! This was the first great victory, which conditioned all subsequent Christian history to this very day.

It conditioned also our *interpretation* of this history, especially its beginnings. We cannot read the New Testament without thinking of those "little flocks" in Galatia, Corinth, Jerusalem, Rome, and other places as the *mere beginnings* of the church. We read about these little fellowships with the eyes of people who know that, later on, these losers were the winners! For us, and for centuries of Christians before us, the destiny of the church in its first few centuries seems an almost classical success story. As Hollywood movie producers have always known, every good success story needs to begin in what seems like failure. What could seem more a failure than that dejected little band which met in the upper room after Jesus' crucifixion! Or those harried little Christian communities in Ephesus and Thessalonica and elsewhere—people buffeted about by the majority, pawns in the hands of the powerful. Mere nobodies, in fact!

But Constantine's Edict of Milan, granting "complete tolerance" to the Christians and restitution of all their lost properties, changed all that. The nobodies became somebodies. Indeed, the last became first! Because the little struggling bands of Christians were faithful to their vision through perseverance and prayer, through patient explanation of their belief to the nonbelieving world, through the inevitability of historical progress, Christianity became the dominant religion of the world. Well, of the Western world at least. And our nineteenth-century Christian forebears devoutly believed the whole world would soon be "conquered for Christ."

This is how we have told our story. Not always so blatantly, of course. But success has been the unmistakable theme all the same. We even turned the story of Jesus into a worldly success story, to correspond with and to provide the basis for our own ecclesiastical story. To such a degree is success the essence of our image of ourselves as Christians that many of us have a hard time conceiving of the church in any other way. Again today, there is on this continent a strong and even militant movement of people who would "win the world for Christ." The church, you see, must win! Everybody must be won over—the whole earth must bow before our God and King. This is how such people conceive the mission of the church in the world; it is how they read the New Testament. They have good precedent for doing so, because it has been done in one way or another for at least sixteen centuries—ever since Constantine provided the sociological grounds for our success story.

At the same time, others among us have noticed something else. They have observed, in these latter days, what happens to Christianity when it becomes a success story. And we are driven by this awareness to reassess this whole interpretation of our history.

The Victims of Success

It has been observed that there are victims of Christian success. I suppose there are some kinds of success which, at least in theory, do not victimize others. The kinds of successes with which the Christian church has usually surrounded itself are not victimless. Success in terms of power, in terms of winning—no matter who achieves it, no matter out of what motivation—always has victims. If one succeeds, it is because another fails. The Crusades of the Middle Ages, and the countless "religious" wars throughout the Christian centuries, have made that truth plain enough. And it is no less true where success does not bring actual bloodshed. If Christ succeeds, the Buddha fails; if Christianity succeeds in the forests of seventeenth-century North America, it is because the Manitou and the spirits of streams and skies and forests fail. There is success for the one, disgrace for the other. And can we be satisfied today, we Christians, with a Christ who throws the Buddha, the Manitou, and all the gods into *disgrace?*

In the past, Christians have been able to cover up the uglier aspects of their successes—or to interpret them as the unfortunate corollary of the progress of the Kingdom of God. More recently the victims of our Christian success have become more conspicuous. We can hardly ignore them any longer. In a society that is no longer "Christian" but is comprised of every sort of religious and nonreligious persuasion—we are made to know it when our evangelism in the community, in schools, in the media, and elsewhere is stepping on somebody else's religious heritage. The victims have become vociferous.

But there is an even more terrible way in which the voices of the victims have spoken to us—at least to all who have ears to hear. For the *great,* historic victims of Christian success have always been the Jews. From the beginning! It is not possible for thinking Christians today to reflect on Auschwitz and the holocaust of Judaism without asking themselves: What was wrong with our story that it gave the possibility of such a "final solution"? To have produced (perhaps even to have *demanded*) these victims, must there not have been something dreadfully wrong with that story? We should not crawl out from underneath this problem by answering that there may indeed have been something wrong with *the German version* of the Christian story. No! It is not so easy as that. The Jews have been made victims in every Christian country in the world. What was wrong with our story is wrong at the heart of it; it does not belong to one or two interpretations only. Perhaps the defect is there already in the New Testament. Perhaps already there one can find the seeds of a story of Christian success that could only become convincing if those people over whom the triumph at the heart of that success was won are themselves pushed aside, thrown into disgrace. What is the "final solution" of the Nazis final in relation to? The answer, alas, is that it is final in relation to a long series of attempts, on the part of a civilization inspired by the Christian success story, to eliminate any symbol of failure. And the Jews, throughout the centuries after Christ, were the most consistent symbol of that failure.

The Price of Success

Not only does success do harmful things to others. Its victims are also those who succeed! A high price must be paid for success, normally a very high one. The price that historic Christianity paid for its worldly success may have been the highest price it could have paid. In order to have prominence, power, and wealth, the church through the centuries had to compromise. To make itself attractive, it had to identify itself with the continuously changing values and goals of whatever empire it sought to win. As the book of Revelation might put it, the Bride of Christ has always had to play the part of the harlot. In exchange for success, it forfeited its identity, its dignity—and perhaps its very soul.

The soul of the church is the gospel. Without that it is nothing. And the gospel is not based on a success story. On the contrary, the story at the heart of the gospel is the tale of a *victim* of success—an unpowerful man, nailed to his cross by successful political, economic, and religious forces. More than that! It is the story of a failure: a young man who, at the age when most young men who are going to "make it" have begun to go places, was put up to die slowly in a public place with a ridiculous sign over his head.

But was it not a success in the long run? I would answer: Yes, if we redefine the term. God did not fail, but his successes are utterly different from what we mean by "success." He could only convey his meaning of victory by putting forward this victim of *our* success! When we turn the victory of the victim into the triumph of the oppressor, we betray the God of the gospel. There is a deep logic in his kind of success, the kind that looks to us like failure. He wants his crucified Son to be there for all who are crucified, for all who suffer. He wants the victims of human power and victory and arrogance to recognize in Jesus another, higher kind of success than that which the world knows. When the church succeeded in worldly terms, and turned its very gospel into a worldly success story, it removed Jesus from the sphere of all who suffer and are victims of human success, all who fail, all who die. That means, finally, that it removed him from the sphere of every human being. For, in the last analysis, none of us is successful in worldly terms. In fact, the whole symbolism of success as this world knows it is a fantastic delusion. In the long run, measured by the standards of that delusive symbol, we all fail.

Another Way

Sometimes—even in middle age!—a crisis in self-understanding brings about a new way of thinking about ourselves that is *better* than the old way. People sometimes really do "improve with age." Coming through these crises of identity, they achieve a more realistic assessment of themselves. They become more human, more modest, more open to others.

Something like that can happen to the church today, if we let it. If we open ourselves to the judgment that begins with the household of God (I Peter 4:17), we might be led to a new and better self-understanding.

Historical providence is giving us this opportunity today. We have allowed ourselves to be swept up into the world's delusions of grandeur—to think of ourselves along the lines of worldly success. Today we are not conspicuously grand, and in countless ways, measured by the standards of success our rather pathetic world still clings to, we have failed. Could we abandon this dream of success once and for all? What could we find in the ruins of Christendom to replace it? Are we prepared to turn to that other way—the way of a success that has all the marks of failure, the way of the cross?

III

THE NEW DIASPORA

As It Was in the Beginning

The New Testament's description of the church parallels, in important ways, our own situation as Christian communities today.

When this awareness begins to dawn on Christians, its impact is very strong. In many ways, it is a new idea and for that reason both exciting and unsettling. Most people do not consider the New Testament's own picture of the church a model for the present. This is because we are trapped in the thought forms of Christendom: we think the New Testament churches were the "mere beginnings."

Still, it seems possible that throughout the ages some Christians sensed an uncomfortable discrepancy between the Biblical description of the church and what it had in fact become. As an adolescent I remember experiencing something similar. Hearing the Bible read in the church service or Sunday school, I would become aware of an enormous difference between the church described in the reading and the circumstances of the congregation listening to it. The gap was particularly conspicuous when the lesson depicted the early church

49

as a suffering community—which, of course, it very often was! The last Beatitude of Jesus is about suffering for the sake of the gospel. The first letter of Peter warns Christians not to be surprised at the "fiery ordeal which comes upon you to prove you, as though something strange were happening to you" (I Peter 4:12). My fellow parishioners listened to such statements as if they understood them fully and were in total agreement with their sentiments. The whole scene sometimes took on for the cynic in me the character of a strange, ironic charade. A comfortable and self-satisfied congregation was hearing itself depicted as rejected by the world, as an alien people in a strange land. That congregation was in reality approximately half of the village assembled for worship (the other half belonged to the other church in town!). By what "world" was the congregation being persecuted? It *was* the world—or half of it, at least.

The little congregations in today's villages and cities are not persecuted by the world either. They are simply ignored by it. Still, there are some important parallels between these "little flocks" and the New Testament churches. There are, of course, some churches that are still full to overflowing, and there one can get the impression that Christendom continues to be the great and glorious thing it always was. But in the more realistic settings of our small congregations today it is possible to feel an astonishing affinity with the church described in the Bible. Our small numbers and our lack of influence make the "little flocks" of the New Testament seem less remote.

This growing sense of "nearness" to the Biblical concept of the church can become the beginning of a new understanding of the nature and mission of the church. The intuitive feeling of many Christians today that we have something fundamental in common with the church of the New Testament, if it is nurtured a little, can be fashioned into a new model of the church. A growing minority of people in the churches are open to such a new model. They have reassessed our Christian past. They have concluded that Christianity turned out to be something different from what Jesus and the original disciple community had in mind. They are not willing to perpetuate the old model of the church any longer. They are looking for a whole new way to think about the church. There is no better place to start this search than the New Testament itself. If we can generate the courage to read the New Testament without bringing all the old presuppositions of Christendom along with us, we can make a highly productive beginning in our attempt to discover an alternative to Christendom.

The Biblical Diaspora

One of the names given to the Christian community of the earliest period is "diaspora" (e.g., I Peter 1:1). It is a Greek word meaning a dispersion, a scattering. Originally the term "diaspora" was applied to the Jews who, just prior to the time of Jesus, had been scattered throughout the countries around the Mediterranean Sea. They were no longer in one place, Palestine, where they formed the majority. Instead, they were minorities in the various countries and cities of the Roman Empire. Later the Christians, too, became grouped in scattered minorities. To begin with, they were far fewer in numbers than the Jews, with whom they were frequently confused by the other members of the society. To be a diaspora meant a number of things for these earliest Christians. Let us concentrate on three of them.

1. Being a diaspora church meant being a *community of belief*. You became a "member" of the Christian fellowship, not by being born into a Christian country, town, or family, but by professing belief in Jesus as the Christ. Of course Christian parents hoped that their children would follow them into belief, or children hoped that their parents would follow *them*. But as Jesus had apparently told his disciples, belief cannot be transferred from one person to another. It will sometimes separate families. One member may believe, the others may not. Fathers and sons, mothers and daughters, friends and friends, will be separated by it. The faith of the church not only unites, it also divides—though it should not utterly alienate persons from one another. At any rate, the only way into the community of belief was through belief. Who else would *want* membership in such a community? There were no fringe benefits! Rather, there were many hazards and deterrents to belief.

The most obvious deterrent to belief was the danger it entailed. Christianity was an "illicit" religion, i.e., it was not legally recognized. One could be punished for belonging to this strange group. Many were punished, and many lost their lives. Even in times of relative toleration, it was not a popular thing to belong to this faith.

There was also another kind of deterrent to belief. Not the external danger; not the struggle with the powers that be; but the internal struggle of faith itself. How could one be sure? It is one thing to be a "believer" when everybody else in society believes, or seems to. It is something else in the diaspora situation. Some people seem to think that the New Testament fellowships were full of totally committed Christians, whose faith contained no shadow of doubt. But this only shows what a distorted view of faith informs our thinking, both inside and outside the churches.

Faith, said Paul, is not sight. It is not the same as absolute certainty. It is not even "total commitment." Like every other human response (e.g., love, hope, courage), faith contains within itself its own opposite: doubt. The prayer of the Christian believer is not: "Lord, I believe; look at my belief—how fully I trust you and accept your every command!" Rather, the Christian prays: "Lord, I believe; help my unbelief." Whoever assumes that there is no unbelief in his or her belief is engaging in self-deception. Belief is a *dialogue* with doubt, not the consequence of overcoming doubt. Genuine faith knows very well the element of unfaith within it, just as genuine love knows its antithesis. Love involves a constant struggle with the unlove and self-love within us. So also faith is an ongoing struggle between our yes and our no to God. Paul describes this struggle in Romans 7. It is a war going on within me. I long for its resolution. I believe that it will one day be resolved, that faith will conquer unfaith. But in the meantime I live with the struggle. I am given the courage to live with it, because I remember that in Jesus the victory has already been achieved.

When we think of the New Testament church as a community of belief, we should not romanticize belief or turn it into a pietistic version of total commitment. It is a matter of dialogue, of a decision taken, not once, but again and again—every day afresh, in fact. Every morning the Christian and the Christian community has to be introduced again to the struggle of faith. And this *internal* struggle is every bit as demanding as the struggle with those external forces in society which are opposed to this religion.

2. The diaspora church of the first centuries of the Christian era was a *movement*. The earliest Christians didn't even call themselves "church," let alone "the church." That came later. They thought of themselves, rather, as the people of "the Way." They were in transit; they were moving.

That meant that they regarded themselves as being "on the right track," going in the right direction. There is always a danger of pride in that assumption, wherever it is found. In fact, their greatest temptation was to think themselves on the right way—with the corollary that the others were going in the wrong direction. Some of the most outspoken passages of the New Testament are written against this kind of presumption—e.g., I Corinthians 9 and 10, and the famous "letters to the churches" in the opening chapters of Revelation.

The other side of the concept attests to a great modesty. For to be "on the way" means not to have arrived. The greatest form of presumptuousness in human beings is not the idea of being on the right track, but the idea of having already arrived. This form of pride was denied the early Christians by their very conception of themselves as being "on the way." They were moving toward a goal, a Kingdom, an ultimate victory. They had not arrived there. That would come; but it would come in God's time, and on his terms. It would come, too, full of surprises. The righteous might turn out to be unrighteous, and the apparently unrighteous might be seen as God's elect (as in the great judgment passage in Matthew 25). The first could be last, the last first. There was no guarantee that anyone would "make it"—there was only the promise that the loving shepherd would not abandon his sheep. The characteristic attitude of the community of faith is therefore not the presumption of having arrived, but the modesty of hope.

This is what I mean by calling the earliest form of Christianity a movement. A movement is not an institution. Most institutions, it is true, began as movements. They started out in modest ways, with some excitement, some sense of adventure. Then they became organized, settled, bureaucratized—in short, institutionalized. Someone said that the best way to kill an idea is to organize it.

In a way, that is what happened to the church. In time it stopped thinking of itself as a movement. It became an organization, eventually one of the greatest organizations this world has ever known—with all the baggage thereto appertaining! The church lost the art of traveling light. It became difficult for the church to move. In the beginning it *had* to travel light, because it had little to call its own. More than that, it was imbued with the sense that its Lord was out front, ahead of it, looking into all the dark corners of earth and beckoning it to follow. The church could only follow if it were flexible, ready to pick up its cross at a moment's notice!

The fundamental idea behind the church's self-understanding as a *diaspora* is the concept that the Christian community is dispersed into all the world as it follows its Lord. The dispersion is not accidental. It is part of the divine plan. It is of the essence of the Christian mission. The church can only engage in its mission if it is on the move, dispersed.

3. The diaspora church was a _minority_, consisting of "little flocks" here and there. What are we to think about this fact? If we develop some of the courage and imagination that I think we need as Christians today, we shall begin to regard the minority status of the early Christian church in *a positive way.* We have come to think "littleness" a disadvantage only because that is how Constantinian Christianity has conditioned us to think. But if we try to approach the New Testament's description of the church without the dubious benefits of Constantinian assumptions, we may be able finally to give a positive content to the conception of the church as a minority.

Did Jesus intend his "church" to become the enormous, world-embracing institution that it did in fact become? Did Jesus ever, in his wildest dreams, think of anything comparable to the Holy Roman Empire? I seriously doubt it.

For one thing, if he had been thinking big, he would surely have used different language in depicting his disciple community. All the metaphors he employed suggest a minority. He said that his followers would be like a bit of yeast in a loaf of bread. He compared them to a candle in the night, set on a candlestick, not under a bushel—but still, only a candle, not a great beacon. He said they would be like salt—a pinch of salt in an otherwise insipid plateful of food. He thought of the little hilltop towns of his country, whose tiny lamps provided some guidance to travelers at night. We heard the word "city" and we thought, naturally, of our great modern cities: New York, Los Angeles, Montreal—with their skyscrapers and neon lights! No, Jesus was thinking about a little country town long before the age of electricity. Not a big blaze of light, just a little light in the darkness, a faint glow on the horizon—that is what he had in mind.

In other words: a creative minority. Jesus knew, as all wise persons have always known, that minorities are significant. They do not wield great power in the manner of big government, multinational corporations, or world-conquering religions. But they have influence just the same, and their influence is all the more important precisely because they are *not* big powers. Because of their vigilance for human life and values that the great powers constantly erode, the minorities can keep the powerful majorities from crushing altogether the spirit of criticism, individuality, and nonconformity. They can hold out an alternative way for those who are oppressed by the dominant culture.

If the church through the centuries has so seldom been a truly prophetic voice in society, it is because it chose to be part of the dominant culture. It identified itself with the great powers, in order to have the same kind of power. It chose to be part of the establishment. This did not happen all at once. It came about not as a deliberate act or a once-for-all decision, but through a whole series of little decisions made and big decisions not made. It allowed those aspects of its own gospel and tradition which resisted incorporation into the established order to be pushed aside and forgotten. Over a long period of time—yes, even before Constantine provided the external occasion for the completion of this process—the church accommodated itself to "the world," to the powers that be. It made itself accessible to the establishment, and the establishment was finally quite happy to welcome it.

Constantine was undoubtedly aware of what an "ecumenical" religion like Christianity could do to help him hold his disintegrating empire together. There were great advantages to be had from it. And every empire ever since has known how to tap Christianity for the good things it could get from this religion. Come and bless our endeavors! Lend your unifying presence to our quest for authority! Conduct for us devotions in high places, prayer breakfasts, memorial services, so that the people will know that God is on our side, backing our power with his almighty power! Be beside us, a great spiritual force, so that all the world will know that we are not the materialistic, grasping, imperialistic empire that we are accused of being! Come, dear Christians, bless our endeavors, our programs, our scientific enterprises, our battleships, munitions factories, and wars!

The church throughout the ages has shown precious little resistance to that invitation. It has come running, cap in hand, at the behest of the powerful. Hence it could hardly be expected to provide a prophetic and creative criticism of worldly power. Only a minority, living outside the king's house, could be vigilant for the king's subjects. Jesus knew that. That is why the community he envisaged as his witnessing community in the world is described by him in the metaphors and language of a minority.

The People of the Cross

The diaspora church of the New Testament knew itself to be a community of *suffering:* the people of "the Way" means the people of the cross. The Way is the way of the cross, the *Via Dolorosa.* How could it be otherwise? The logic of the three characteristics of the diaspora church we have just reflected on points inevitably to suffering as the *most* characteristic feature of the Christian community. To be a community of *belief* means to believe in a Christ despised and rejected by the official society. To be a *movement* means to share with Christ his lack of a place to lay his head, to rest, to build tabernacles. To be a *minority* means to be a critical minority, announcing the judging love of God in the midst of a tottering civilization. All this adds up to suffering. And the earliest Christians didn't expect anything else, except when they forgot themselves and had to be reminded (by Paul and others) that at the very center of their gospel there was a man despised, rejected, broken:

> We preach Christ crucified, a stumbling block to the religious and foolishness to the worldly-wise.
> (I Cor. 1:23f., paraphrased)

Not a hero; not a Promethean type of sufferer, either; rather, a human being whose identification with suffering humanity was so complete and selfless that faith could perceive in it the suffering at the very heart of God. It was this man and this God with whom the Christians were being identified, to whose life and death they were being "conformed." Therefore suffering was their natural lot. This was so not because they sought it—they were not masochists. But, following the Lord whom they were called to follow, and with him identifying themselves with suffering humanity, they could not avoid the cross in one form or another.

The New Testament is full of this theme, this insistence. Luther became aware of it, in a way that few Christians are aware, and he concluded, on the strength of this Biblical theme, that the one mark of the church which must never be lost is (as he put it) "the mark of the holy cross." In other words, all the other traditional marks of the church may be in doubt, hidden, or even lost; its unity, its catholicity, its holiness, its apostolicity, all may be lost, or at least obscured. But when the church loses the mark of the cross, when it ceases to be a community of suffering, it is simply no longer the church. If you want to find the church then, you must look elsewhere. The true church will be a place where people suffer—not masochistically, not in self-indulgence and self-pity, but because of their identification with a suffering Lord and a suffering world!

This insistence of Luther's, that the mark of the cross is essential, is a true summary of the theme of suffering central to the whole Bible, and is the most neglected element of the Scriptural picture of the church. It is inevitable that it should have been neglected by a church which, throughout at least sixteen long centuries, became so identified with the dominant, powerful elements of worldly society that it could not be in solidarity either with a suffering God or the suffering, oppressed elements of human civilization. If little real suffering has been demanded of the mainline churches of our world, it is no wonder. Constantinian Christianity, whether in its legally established form or in our North American form of cultural establishment, has been "spared" the ignominy and brokenness of the New Testament *koinōnia.* But at what cost?

Today we have come to the end of that Constantinian era. At such a time, we can no longer ignore this one essential "mark" that is presented by the writers of the New Testament and recognized by a few throughout the history of Christianity as being indispensable to the church. To take the New Testament church as our model—and to do so with great seriousness—means above all to recognize that we shall have to suffer. This, I feel quite certain, will increasingly become the lot of the church of the future. But it is already our lot, too, if we are able at all to discern the signs of the times. And we are ill-prepared for such a way of life as the way of the cross!

But What About "World Mission"?

Many Christians upon hearing this kind of description of the church are frankly disturbed. They are disturbed at the prospect of becoming a suffering people in the world—though for the most part they do not speak about that. But they do raise a more theoretical question. They want to know: "What about world mission, then?" Did not Jesus say, "Go ye into all the world, and preach the gospel to every creature" (Mark 16:15)? Is it not the responsibility of the church to attempt to convert the whole world to Christ—or at least to *attempt* it? What, otherwise, are we to make of such a command as the one found at the end of Matthew's account:

Go ye therefore, and teach all nations, baptizing
them in the name of the Father, and of the Son, and
of the Holy Ghost: Teaching them to observe all
things whatsoever I have commanded you; and lo,
I am with you alway, even unto the end of the
world. Amen. (Matt. 28:19–20)

This does indeed seem pretty straightforward. (I have
quoted from the King James Version because this is,
interestingly enough, still the language most commonly
associated with the "world mission" concept.) After
centuries of hearing it under the conditions of Christendom and with all the assumptions of Constantinian
Christianity, the meaning of "the Great Commission"
seems all the more clear-cut to us today. Since Christianity became the official religion of the Roman Empire
(and to some extent even before that), the church has
conceived of its task as a universal mission to "convert
the heathen." Its dominant thought about itself has not
been that of a minority called to witness to an alternative "Way." Rather, it has pictured itself throughout
most of its history as the earthly agent of an omnipotent
God. Through its activity the entire world should be
confronted with the divine truth revealed in Jesus
Christ and, by one means or another, caused to bow to
this one and only Lord and Savior of the race, and to
confess that Jesus Christ is Lord (Phil. 2:10f.).

Understanding this as its mandate from Almighty
God, the church was able in good conscience to use all
kinds of tactics to bring about the conversion of unbelievers. It did not flinch even at the use of deceit,
bribery, and physical force—though its methods were
frequently less barbarous and sometimes gentle. So
powerful was this sense of "world mission" that sincere

Christians could imagine, when they went about putting stubborn unbelievers to terrible torture or wrong believers to death, that they were strictly about the loving business of their God. After all, it was better for the pagan or the heretic to suffer in this life than to be damned eternally!

Modern Christian groups that are still imbued with this sense of the need to convert the whole world to Christ have dispensed with the more gruesome aspects of that vocation. Yet the same psychic attitude and the same imperial fervor can be found among them still. They will not resort to torture as a method of conversion, but they will certainly resort to powerful psychological forms of persuasion. Modern technological society has provided them with far more excellent tools than the crude instruments dreamed up in the primitive cellars of the Inquisition! Moreover, if these modern Christians are criticized for appealing to the emotions and using mass hysteria or subtle indoctrination, they will offer in their own defense the same response as the medieval inquisitors gave: it is better to use such methods to bring people to Christ than to let them go damned into the future. One such group, presently active in North America and elsewhere, speaks about "divine deceit." The theory is that afterward, i.e., after the convert has been helped to make the breakthrough into faith, such a person will be open to a more reasonable explication of what is involved in Christian belief.

All of this stems from the centuries-old assumption that it was the intention of our Lord to create a church that embraced the entire universe. Some versions of this were unqualifiedly universalistic: all people everywhere would *eventually* be won for Christ. Other versions (perhaps the majority) have been informed by the kind of predestinarian theology which assumed that while all must be *called* to belief, only some would believe. While this idea appears more modest than the universalist version, in reality it is just as presumptuous; it assumes that *Christianity* is the ultimate truth by which all humanity is judged.

In whatever version the assumption has appeared, it has tried to justify itself on Biblical grounds. Proof texts of various kinds can be found to justify almost any historical version of this assumption. The last two verses of Matthew's Gospel are, in a way, the chief Scriptural cornerstone for the whole attitude. But more refined texts, proving universalist assumptions, or proving the assumptions of "double predestination," can also be unearthed. There are even quite powerful groups within Christendom today which know to the man (or woman?) precisely how many people are going to make it into the heavenly Kingdom!

The need for "proving" all this is itself an interesting phenomenon. If it is so obvious that Christianity has the right and responsibility under God of turning the whole world to Christ, why has so much of exegetical energy been spent defending that idea, or special versions of it? It is not, after all, an *obvious* Biblical concept. In fact, it conflicts seriously with the picture of the New Testament church as the diaspora church. The discrepancy between the New Testament community of suffering and the world-conquering church of "Christendom" is striking. In order to prove itself the legitimate successor of the New Testament beginnings, Christendom has to engage in a prodigious amount of rationalization. This rationalization has usually taken the form of Biblical "exegesis" or interpretation for the precise reason that the Bible itself is the greatest critic, finally, of the whole notion of a world "conquered for Christ"! We are all captivated by that notion, at least at the emotional level, because, in the first place, it is a powerful and appealing psychological concept. In the second place, there have been sixteen centuries of conditioning! It is a highly human reaction to think that what one believes and values is so right and necessary that everyone in the world should believe and value it! For most of its history the Christian church has been able to apply this highly human reaction to its own version of absolute truth. It is not surprising that we all stand in awe of the notion, even today. It is indeed so powerful among us still that many in the older denominations have deep feelings of inferiority because our churches have not been as successful as the newer, more zealous, formerly "sectarian" groups at bringing the world to Christ.

But I, for one, am more and more convinced that the whole assumption of "world mission" according to that understanding of it is false. In fact, it is a gross misunderstanding, an ironic and even pathetic misappropriation of the teaching of our Lord and of his disciples. Let me explain what I mean.

No doubt it was the intention of Jesus and the original disciple community that the "word of the cross" should be preached throughout the *oikoumenē* (the inhabited world). Everybody should hear this gospel of the judging, redeeming love of God. This sense of urgency obviously informed the whole life of the early church. It is behind the mission of Paul to the Gentiles. It is bound up with the apocalyptic sense of the early Christians— the feeling that the end is very near. Before the end, everyone should at least hear these good tidings. Shout the news from the housetops! Go, tell it on the mountains!

However, it is a long way from this sense of evangelism which informed the New Testament diaspora to the enforced baptisms of the post-Constantinian years or the manipulative "mass evangelism" of today. The difference can be stated in three observations:

1. The Biblical witnesses never imagined that many would believe the message of salvation. In fact, they assumed that it would be only a few. Jesus himself, on at least one occasion, pondered whether, at the time of the end, when the Son of Man would return in glory, there would be any belief at all on earth. The minority concept is upheld throughout the Biblical material.

2. The "little flocks" were nevertheless not to be discouraged. God's grace and the salvation brought through Christ, they believed, was at work in the world in spite of mankind's unbelief—in spite also of their own unbelief! In God's own time the world would perceive that God had been at work in Jesus for its redemption. Yes, in that last time (not now!) every knee would bow and every tongue confess that Jesus Christ is Lord. And this brings us to the third observation.

3. The diaspora church made a sharp distinction between the Kingdom of God and themselves. The church is not the Kingdom in New Testament theology. No doubt the church is *related to* the Kingdom, in the sense that it is a witness to the presence of the Kingdom, and is itself the product of this presence. But it is not to be equated with the Kingdom. The Kingdom about which Jesus speaks is far broader, more inclusive, and above all more mysterious than the church. "Many

whom God has," said Augustine, "the church does not have; and many whom the church has, God does not have." In other words, there is in the New Testament the sense of an "invisible church" (as the Reformers later called it). The visible church, the little flocks here and there, are only tokens of the Kingdom of God in its mysterious totality. They are not even *necessarily* part of the Kingdom, as the famous "letters to the churches" in the book of Revelation make quite clear. The passage from church to Kingdom is at least as hard as the passage from world to Kingdom—perhaps even more so, because the church has been given greater awareness of the Kingdom and therefore possesses greater responsibility. "Every one to whom much is given, of him will much be required" (Luke 12:48).

It is the responsibility of the church to bear witness to the presence of the Kingdom—not in itself, but in the world at large. Jesus Christ the King, the crucified King, is at work throughout human society. His Spirit is loose in the world. The church is to identify this Spirit, and to identify itself with the work of the triune God in God's beloved world. It is not the business of the church to turn the world *into church*. It is the church's business, rather, to point to the presence in and throughout the world of the King who is turning the world into his Kingdom. And let us remember that *his* Kingdom is so utterly unlike the "kingdoms of this world" that even the church, which is always tempted to seek the power of the worldly kingdoms, must be constantly astonished at the places and the ways in which it breaks into human history. Not at all predictable is this King, least of all if we think of him as a king!

There are strains of thought in the New Testament

which can suggest a more direct equation of church and Kingdom, which insinuate that the church should expand in a universal way. Some passages, at any rate, seem to do that. But it is hard to overestimate the extent to which we read the New Testament through eyes that have been trained to look for certain things—Constantinian eyes, as we may say. Today there is a better opportunity to discover what the New Testament actually says. This opportunity is present, not only because we have better tools of historical scholarship, but, more important than that, because we are questioning many of the assumptions with which, until now, this collection of writings has been read by the church. Wherever the church realizes that the Christendom model no longer really pertains, it is open to doubt whether the New Testament ever *wanted* the Christendom model to pertain!

In this new spirit of inquiry, texts about the universal mission of the church need to be studied again. For a long time, Biblical scholars have been telling us that elements of these particular texts, Mark 16:15 and Matt. 28:19–20, are later additions to the original (no one is quite sure how late they are). But we have not been in a position heretofore to listen seriously to these scholars because we wanted to think of ourselves as belonging to a conquering faith. *The* religious success of all time! But knowing ourselves to be something less than a success today, and suspecting the whole concept of success, we can perhaps begin to listen and to consider the internal criticism of the New Testament against these pretensions to world domination. If we do turn to the New Testament with such questions in our minds, what we shall find there by way of a model of the church is not

this world-conquering "Christendom" that still operates in our midst as a powerful and persuasive symbol
of the church, but a diaspora: little flocks here and
there, witnessing to the love of God—a love that is not
only broader than the measure of human minds, but
broader than *the church's* understanding and appropriation of it.

IV

LIVING ON THE BOUNDARY

What we have said thus far may be summed up as follows. *First,* we are living at the end of the great period of Christian dominance in the Western world—the end of Christendom. However, if we have ears to hear, we can develop the courage to see this as the beginning of the church—a new beginning. *Second,* in this state of mind many of us in the churches today are open to a reassessment of the Christian past. We are ready to entertain radical questions about the meaning of that past, about the rightness and wrongness of many of the church's deeds and assumptions—including its image of itself as a triumphing religious institution, a "mighty army." *Third,* we are also open to the future in a new way. Because we not only sense the end of what the church has been in the past but also question the rightness of what it has been, we are ready to entertain a new image of the church. And the best new image is in fact not so very new after all. It is the basic one that we already find in the New Testament, provided we do not read the New Testament with too many of the assumptions of "Christendom." This is the model of the church as diaspora—little groupings of Christians here and there, like a bit of yeast, a pinch of

70

salt, a little light, witnessing to something bigger and much more inclusive.

Reluctance to Change

A significant minority of church people today are ready to explore the possibilities of littleness, of being a diaspora. We know that we cannot go on in the old way any longer. We know that we must change, and radically so. We are ready for quite fundamental change—more so today than ten or twenty years ago, when most of the changes made were superficial. We know that the change which is needed must be radical: a change at the roots of things, a change of our very self-understanding; a change in our way of thinking about ourselves and our place as Christians in the human community. We are ready for this . . .

And yet we hesitate.

In part, our hesitation is sinful, and we know it. It is the hesitation of people who are afraid of change. Who wants to be an Abraham, going out to some place, any place—destination unknown! The model of the church on which we have been reared and which is part of our emotional equipage is strong within us. It is a comfortable and in some ways an exhilarating model. We have been rich, and now we don't want to become poor. We have been safe, and we want (humanly enough!) to remain safe. We have been in charge—nobody's slaves, nobody's inferiors! Who wants to become little after all that? Who wants to leave the beauty and comfort and even grandeur of our old home in Christendom for some arid wilderness—or for slavery in somebody else's house!

We know all that is sinful—a matter of inertia, of straightforward disobedience. But it is strong in us, and the powers of rationalization and repression are strong, too.

On the other hand, some of our hesitation is legitimate and right, or at least justifiable. At the roots of this aspect of our hesitancy is a kind of wariness about the new model of the church that is being proposed to us. After all, every conception of the church has its dangers. This one, surely, is no exception. It can go wrong. It can become just as questionable as the old imperialistic, world-conquering concept of the church on which we lived for sixteen centuries.

There are two dangers, in particular, that cause us to hesitate in relation to the diaspora model of the church. They are two sides of the same coin.

Lost in the Crowd

On the one side there is the danger of being lost in the crowd. How could a Christian church that had determined to be immersed in the life of the world as small, scattered communities prevent itself from being swallowed up? Would it have a voice at all? Would it not simply be co-opted by the majority culture? Our technological society is capable of taking all kinds of seemingly prophetic and deviant elements into itself, and rendering them harmless through its inclusive embrace. How could the church avoid the fate of so many other minorities, with their seemingly different "alternatives"? Wouldn't the distinctively *Christian* nature of this community simply disappear, in time, or be so mixed with other ideas, other ideologies and programs for reform, that it would become just one small ingredient in the stew—not even salt, but just an indistinct, overboiled bit of vegetable matter?

The more such a church attempted to model itself on the diaspora concept, would it not that much more run the risk of being assimilated into the general cultural milieu? Let us suppose that the church really tried, for example, to stop being "institutional"; tried to become a movement again—the people of the Way. With this in mind, it gets rid of a great deal of its institutional baggage, too heavy for the sort of travel to which it is now called: its properties, its elaborate bureaucracies, its mountainous circulations of printed materials, its expensive conferences, perhaps most of its paid workers. Like a traveler at sea in the midst of a storm, it throws all these things overboard to save what is essential. But in the process might it not lose its very essence? Save its skin but lose its soul? Might it not become so totally bereft of anything really *distinctive* to say and do in the world that the world would find it neither a threat nor a promise, but only something boring and insipid that it would either spit out altogether or else digest easily along with everything else, and not even notice?

There are historical precedents for thinking this a danger. Already in the New Testament, as we know particularly from the letters of Paul, some Christians were behaving in such "worldly" ways that the apostles had to remind them that they were called to be different—not "of the world." Recent history has also provided more than a few instances of Christian individuals and groups who tried so much to be in the world in a serving and nonmanipulative way that many of them were finally indistinguishable from the wallpaper.

The Holy Clique

The second danger is the other side of this same coin, because it always emerges as a reaction to the first danger. Sensing that there is a good chance of being lost in the crowd, Christian minorities have often said to one another: Listen! Instead of being submerged in this indifferent stew of human society, let us draw a circle around ourselves and be separate, different. Let us be distinctively *Christian!*

This mentality has inspired many movements in historical Christianity, some of them laudable in many respects. Sometimes they kept the faith alive in a way that it would not have been preserved otherwise. I am thinking of the monastic movement, pietism in the late Middle Ages, some of the communal movements coming out of the Reformation of the sixteenth century. What these movements had to fight against was not a pagan or secular culture, but a culture that pretended to be Christian and announced itself as such. Against this cultural Christianity, faithful and devout Christians insisted that the faith of the Christ should not be identified with the values and aspirations of human societies, nor the glory of God with the kingdoms of this world and the glory of them.

This way constitutes a danger all the same. We sense it as we think about the diaspora model of the church. For all the insistence of the New Testament that the Christian community is not to be "of the world," there is an equal insistence that it be decidedly and concretely *in* the world. In fact, the only reason for not being "of the world" is that thereby the church may be

the more effectively "in the world"—as salt, as yeast, as
light. To hive off from the world, to be a ghetto, to exist
as a fine, pious, and peaceable fellowship of Christians
living in isolation from the rest of humanity with its
unrest and its malaise—this is not the destiny of the
church which truly follows in the steps of its Lord. The
danger of being a holy clique has always been present
in the church. It is particularly present whenever Christians
feel that they are a minority. It is therefore a great
danger today, and many Christian groups have already
fallen into it. We hesitate, therefore, to take up a model
of the church in which such a danger is conspicuously
present.

So we ask: Is there any guarantee that one or the
other of these two dangers will not engulf the church
which takes up that model? How can we ensure that the
diaspora church will not fall into the trap of being lost
in the crowd, on the one hand, or becoming a ghetto on
the other? How can the church walk the tightrope between these two temptations?

Living on the Boundary

The answer to such questions is that there is no guarantee of anything at all. The church has always fallen
into dangers in the past. Likely it will continue to do so.
We should not get into the habit of thinking that, just
because we may have come to the end of a long and
questionable version of Christianity, the church that
will now emerge from the ashes of old Christendom will
be something pure and spotless! A pure and spotless
church is in the first place a contradiction in terms. The
church of Jesus Christ is a community of sinners whose

only real virtue is that they have learned—or begun to learn—how to confess their sin and start again. The emergent church will not be completely new, free from the sins of the fathers, free from its own sin! But a fresh start can be made. The church will not then be perfect —one knows that from the outset. But perhaps it can be a little different. Perhaps we can learn from past mistakes, at least a little!

To start with, we might learn what it means to risk. To *risk the dangers!* We know they are there, and so we hesitate. It is natural. But our hesitation is also a decision. It means we are deciding—by not deciding—to remain the way we are: a mishmash of denominational institutions living, luxuriously, as if it were still yesterday. A hangover from the heyday of Christendom, seeming to be brave but in reality merely pathetic. The fact is, we cannot remain as we are. Time and history are changing us—yes, God himself, I think, is changing us. We have either to *decide* to change, in which case we will be permitted to have some say in our future, or else we will be changed without being consulted, in which case all eternity will judge us to have been not merely hesitant but cowardly.

You have only to look at the gray heads and empty pews in so many of the churches of our major denominations to grasp, in a graphic way, my meaning. Sometimes I have the impression that T. S. Eliot's famous line about the world ending "not with a bang but a whimper" applies quite literally to the old churches of Christendom. Wisely, we are not ready to get on the bandwagon of the new, crass versions of Constantinian Christianity that are supposed to be sweeping this continent. But because we are so cautious and afraid, we sit on our hands and wait for the undertaker of history to close our doors for us, and wire them shut, and leave them to rot in the elements. Or, if they are interesting enough architecturally, somebody may write "Museum" over the entrances.

Regarding the question posed by the title of this book, I think that the church *does* have a future. But the *kind* of future it has will depend, in significant measure, upon how we act right now. By "we" I mean, in a particular way, we Christians of the old mainline Protestant, Catholic, and Orthodox churches.

To risk something different from what historical Christianity has already tried for centuries means to believe that the tightrope can be walked! We are called to believe today that it really is possible to be a diaspora church without falling into the oblivion of nonidentity within the pluralistic society or, on the other hand, retreating into a religious ghetto. To put it positively—and to introduce another metaphor—we are called to believe that it is possible to live on the boundary: the boundary between time and eternity; the boundary between the word of God and the word of man; the boundary between Christ and culture; the boundary between gospel and newspaper; the boundary between being "in the world" and not being "of the world." There are many ways to speak about the boundary. They all mean that the Christian community is called to be a movement which lives within the structures of this world, but which brings to these structures a judgment and a hope transcending them.

Isn't this where the church has always been called to live—on the boundary? Isn't this in fact what it means to be the church? The internal logic of the whole thing is that there should be in the world a colony of human beings, a remnant, and a witnessing community that for all its own worldliness is yet enabled from time to time to bear witness to a meaning, a hope, which is not the world's product but is precisely its intended destiny.

If I were God (which by great fortune I am not!) and I wanted to communicate my love to a world that turned its back on me, what sort of messenger would I send? Surely not a messenger who found the message so precious that he wanted to keep it for himself—or keep it from being tainted and maybe lost in the midst of all the other noises of the world. And surely not a messenger who became so interested in the world that he allowed himself to forget the message. No, I would need somebody who could achieve both things: a profound understanding of and respect for the message, and a deep involvement in and commitment to the life of the world. Without understanding and respect for the integrity of the message, there can be nothing for the messenger to communicate. Without involvement in the life of the world, there can be no real communication.

Again and again in its history the church has fallen to one or the other side. The dominant forms of Christianity became so immersed in the world that they had no message to bring. The purist forms of Christianity became so ghettoized that they couldn't communicate with the world even if they had something important to say. Nevertheless the command to live on the boundary has always been there. It is part of the Biblical witness; it belongs to the story that is told in both Testaments.

If we hear this command today in an urgent way,

knowing that we stand at a decisive crossroads in Christian existence, it is not altogether new. The same command has always been given to the people of God in the world. On the one hand they are beckoned to come away from the world: "Come out from them, and be separate from them" (II Cor. 6:17); "Do not be conformed to this world" (Rom. 12:2); "You are not of the world" (John 15:19). On the other hand, they are sent into the world and commanded to be "in the world" in a way that even the most worldly of human beings are not in it, in solidarity with its pain and its longing. The Christian community is beckoned away from the love of temporal things and toward the love of things eternal —to the end that it may love "the neighbor"! These are two sides of *the same life.* Each side is dependent upon the other. Separated, they produce distortions of the church; and the history of the church is the history of these distortions. Nevertheless, it is possible to begin *again.* It is possible to try—this time in quite new historical circumstances—to keep the two sides together; to live on the boundary between them.

No Fence-Sitting!

But let us mark well: Living on the boundary does not mean sitting on the fence! Every theology can be turned into an excuse for something questionable. The danger of the theology of life on the boundary is that it sometimes leads to fence-sitting. This happens when the church says that it cannot become wholly involved with some worldly cause because it has to maintain its loyalty to the "things eternal." So it will go a little way with one who asks it to walk a mile. Then it becomes nervous and hesitant and conditional. "We must maintain our loyalty to God, to the gospel, to the Spirit. So we cannot go all the way with you, dear friend." But Jesus said: "If anyone forces you to go one mile, go with him two miles" (Matt. 5:41). And the Samaritan in Jesus' parable went all the way with the one who fell among thieves. No doubt in order to do so he had to compromise some of his other loyalties, including his religious loyalties!

The call to live on the boundary should not be interpreted as a rationale for fence-sitting, especially not at the ethical level. The church of the future will be asked to go a long way—more than the second mile—with persons and groups who live far away from the boundary. It must go. There is no alternative. Even at the risk of losing everything! Even at the risk of not remembering the message! The call of God is never to preserve correct doctrine but to preserve life. Those who lose their souls in the preservation of someone else's soul will gain what they have lost. But those who would save their own lives will lose them.

In other words, if it comes to a showdown between unworldliness and being "in the world," it is always the latter that must be chosen by a faithful church. Even if the church loses something of its gospel; even if it compromises something of its ultimate loyalty to its Lord, it is bound to remain with the world God loves. Better that the church of the future should come out as a neighbor to the one who fell among thieves (which is the state of the human race in our time) than that it should come out as a loyal priest who didn't want to compromise his ultimate loyalty to God, and therefore neglected bruised and bleeding humanity.

Wherever there seems to be a conflict of loyalties between God and his human creatures, between this side of the border and that, the Christian decision must always be to serve humanity. This is the meaning of the incarnation. This is the gospel of the cross. It is the courage to risk our own salvation for the sake of our neighbor; the courage to believe that if we are loyal to the neighbor we will never be far from the love of God.

This is the norm that we must take with us as we move to the discussion of ways in which the diaspora church may relate to others, including other human agencies, other causes, and other religious traditions, in the world that is coming to be.

V

QUESTIONS WE FACE

We are faced by so many questions we don't even know what half of them are. We have been accustomed to living in the world as its religious presence, its conscience, its official priest. We simply take for granted a great many things that cannot be taken for granted any longer. We assume that some things are ours by right; that it is our very duty to uphold them. We still behave according to patterns that were established centuries ago; the greatest share of them are outmoded, some of them are so obsolete as to be ludicrous. A symbol of the latter is the courtroom practice of swearing on the Bible. We are just now beginning to be conscious of some of the questions that confront us as Christians today. We are still ignorant of many questions, not to speak of answers!

Therefore, I cannot pretend to take on all the kinds of questions that the church faces as it attempts to embrace a different mode of being in the world. But I want to try, in a modest way, to address three broad areas of relationship between church and world which may be among the most significant of the relationships in which, as Christians, we stand. In the process, it may be possible to depict further the diaspora model of the church to which I have been pointing.

The three areas of relationship between church and world to which I intend to speak are: (1) government; (2) movements and causes that sometimes parallel Christian concern; and (3) other religions.

From House Chaplain to Prophet

Even before Constantine brought the Christian church into his imperial house and commanded its leaders to govern the spiritual side of the body politic, Christians were making gestures of friendliness toward the ruling authorities. Paul, in the thirteenth chapter of Romans (surely one of the most unfortunate pieces of writing in the Bible), admonished the Christians:

> Let every soul be subject unto the higher powers. For there is no power but of God: the powers that be are ordained of God. Whosoever therefore resisteth the power, resisteth the ordinance of God: and they that resist shall receive to themselves damnation. (Rom. 13:1–2)

Paul, I am sure, would have destroyed that part of his letter to the "little flock" in Rome if he had been able to look into the future. Especially if he had seen how Christians in Germany in the 1920's and 1930's used this very statement to justify Adolf Hitler's coming to power. Similarly, I suspect that the author of the First Letter of Peter would have conditioned his "Fear God, honor the king" (I Peter 2:17) had he known the extent to which God and king would become inextricably bound up with each other in the minds of ordinary people. Those who resisted tyrants like King John of

England, for example, wresting from him the Magna Carta, could only do so in mortal terror of damning their eternal souls.

The Christian apologists of the second century addressed the rulers of Rome. They wanted to explain themselves, to interpret the faith, to defend the church against erroneous and sometimes silly charges and rumors. Sometimes they also came close to currying favor. And there were always those in the early centuries who sought greater proximity to power, or even the establishment of the faith. We ought not to blame Constantine alone for what came to be. The Christians for their part were prepared for his invitation. There was little resistance, so far as I am aware, when Constantine invited them to become the priests of his empire and his personal house chaplains.

All the same, the early Christian attempts to mollify power were understandable, and those attempts were different from what happened later on. They were understandable because the Christians did have to identify themselves and explain what they truly were. They were not simple anarchists or revolutionaries. They did pray for the wise use of power by those who held it. They did render to Caesar the things that belonged to Caesar. Living outside the official culture, as an illegal and—in the best of times—only slightly tolerated minority, the Christian communities of the early church did have to explain themselves to those who held power.

But after they were brought into the palaces of the governing powers to function as house chaplains, they went far beyond this kind of explanation. Indeed, the church soon began to think itself the spiritual wing of the state. It became jealous of that role and quickly excluded all others from having any part in it. During the time of the emperor Theodosius the Great, who was converted to Christianity in A.D. 380, all other religions were declared illegal. A little more than half a century after the formerly illegal Christians had become the house chaplains of the Empire, they had successfully excluded all other candidates for that office. Having come into proximity to power, they adapted to the power mentality quickly, and uncritically.

We may not be far wrong to generalize, historically, and say that with few exceptions precisely that situation has pertained ever since. We may even go farther and observe that still today the great bulk of Christians in our world know no other way of being vis-à-vis the state than to seek the closest possible proximity to it and to use to the hilt the power that comes through this proximity.

What this attitude has meant concretely can be summed up in two closely related observations. On the one hand it has meant that the normal attitude toward the state on the part of the Christian church, whether in old, formally established situations such as England and Germany, or in the New World, is to support the policies and practices of the government. The church has functioned primarily as the legitimizer of the state. The best way to prove this historical generalization is to note what happens here and there when representatives of the church become critical of government in a fundamental way—or even practice civil disobedience. Figures like the Berrigan brothers—antiwar activists who destroyed draft board records—were extremely offensive to those in power, not just because of *what* they did, but because they were clergy doing it! The clergy, even if they are dissenters within their own ecclesiastical communion, are supposed to be house chaplains in relation to the state. When they act against the government, they betray this well-established image of the church, so many centuries in the building. It is as if a trusted member of the family had betrayed the other members.

One consequence of being the house chaplain is that the church is obligated to support its host, the state. The other side of this same coin is that the church believes it has certain rights within the body politic. An intimate member of the royal household should have some privileges, after all! Or at least some fringe benefits. The church should not have to beg in its own house. There should be a certain mutuality of support.

This expectation of state support on the part of the Christian church has led to many nefarious and evil things. The sword has not been spared by the state in protecting its chaplain! We are now a little more humane, perhaps, or a little more subtle. Partly because the church can no longer *expect* such clear-cut protection from government. All the same, the carry-over of the power relationship is still very much with us. In their approaches to the state, the churches almost invariably manifest this deeply entrenched attitude. They do not come in the modest way of servants, or in the prophetic way of guardians of humanity. They come as honored members of the family. They do not feel any special compunction to let their cause stand on its own merits. They should be listened to because they are churches! They have rights! The word "rights" comes almost automatically to the lips of house-chaplain Christians. In the province of Quebec today, the "anglophone" Christians on the whole do not find it necessary to reason their way through their statements to a government they find hostile to their cause. Certainly they do not think through their briefs and their recommendations *theologically!* They take their stand, rather, on "rights." In this respect they are no different from the other power groups of the English-speaking minority—educators, businessmen, professionals. Like all these other elements of the old economic elite, the Anglo-Saxon churches in Quebec simply assume that they have inalienable rights.

If we move to a different model of the church—the model of the church "in dispersion"—we must find a new way of being vis-à-vis power in general and government in particular. I am certainly not competent to present a blueprint for this new way of being. It has to be found through trial and error, adventure and discovery, corporate and not merely individual thought and planning. At the same time, I do not think that we are left without some precedents—some guidance from our own peculiar sources and from elements in our own past. There is also help to be had from sister churches in parts of the world where the necessity for new ways of thinking have been forced upon Christians in a way that has not happened so dramatically in our context.

Speaking first of our sources, we need to learn in a special way from what we call the "Old Testament" (a way of speaking about the Hebrew Bible which, in my opinion, we should attempt to change). Our return to the Hebrew Bible needs to involve us, at the same time, in a new encounter with the living community of Israel. I suspect that the Jewish interpretation of the Scriptures is more reliable than most Christian representations of the Biblical point of view.

My reasons for this proposal are more complex than I can develop in this place, but one thing at least has to be said. An unfortunate aspect of the earliest forms of Christianity (unfortunate insofar as this question of the relation between church and state is concerned) is that the church in the earliest period of its history was so preoccupied with "the ultimate" that it tended to neglect "the penultimate." To explain: The Christians of the early church were looking for an ultimate, complete transformation of earth by the coming of the heavenly Kingdom. The Lord was to return soon—momentarily! So they tended to be rather cavalier about matters of daily life: sexuality, marriage, family, economics, class structures in society, government. All these things would soon come to an end. Paul's strangely uncritical statement about being subject to the ruling authorities (Romans 13) should be seen in the light of that historical context—what is called the eschatological expectation. Certainly Paul did not think he was laying down guidelines for two thousand years of Christian existence in this world! Consequently these "interim ethics" of the early Christians are not always helpful for a situation—such as ours—where we expect and hope for a continuation of life in this world. We want to know how the church could help to sustain and contribute to civilization.

The Hebrew Bible can and should therefore be turned to for guidance—and the living community of Israel is the best interpreter of that Bible, especially in relation to a question like the present one. To begin with, in the Hebrew Bible we can see a struggle be-

tween the religious and the political realm. It is taken
for granted that there must be political authority. Society—life itself—would not be possible without the "governing authorities." This sense of the importance of
government leads, in the story of Israel, to the establishment of the kingship. The Hebrew Bible affirms that
this is part of God's own providence; and a figure like
King David is and still remains for Judaism a symbol of
God's providential dealing with his people.

At the same time, there was strong criticism of the
kingship from the beginning. Even in the best of times,
prophetic Judaism knew that "power tends to corrupt
and absolute power corrupts absolutely." Some strong
factions within the community of Israel resisted the
establishment of the kingship. Only God is king, they
insisted. There is only one Absolute, and this divine
Absolute cannot be identified with anything temporary
and earthly. The prophets of Israel again and again had
to come before their kings with the message: You have
betrayed your calling. You are not the Absolute, but
only a weak symbol of the Absolute who transcends you.
You have taken for yourself the place of the Absolute—
you, a mere man. You are no longer the shepherd-king,
the protector of the people; you are the wolf who de-
vours them. Thus Nathan said to David: "You are the
man!" (II Sam. 12:7).

This prophetic sense is in fact the great genius of
Hebraic religion in relation to power in general and to
the state in particular. Biblical faith is not anarchistic. It
knows that power is necessary. But unlike Paul in Romans 13, who also knows that power is necessary, Hebraic faith is always suspicious of power. What Alex-
ander Solzhenitsyn said about the good citizen could

have been said by anyone who took the tradition of Jerusalem seriously: A good citizen is someone who has an innate suspicion of power.

Israel, the living, continuing community, has been given reason through these two thousand years of "Christian" power to be even more skeptical about power than it was in the Biblical period. Throughout these centuries, unlike the Christians, the Jews have had to live outside the houses of kings, rulers, and the authoritative elements of the society. For just this reason Israel has played an amazing part in the preservation of humanity. I mean "humanity" in the qualitative sense of that word: Israel has preserved a quality of life, sanity, reason, mercy, learning, humor—against all the powers that would rob humanity of these things. Israel has been unusually vigilant for humanity because it knew deeply from within its own experience that power, if not continually checked, will always tend to rob, truncate, and finally destroy what is truly human.

Here and there in our own Christian past we can find the same lesson. To take one example: We are beginning to be able to read the story of the Reformation today in a new light. The leading Reformers, after their original rebellion against the reigning powers, were themselves co-opted by powers new and old. They became house chaplains in their turn, and—again in their turn—saw to it that the outsiders (in this case the left-wing Reformers like Thomas Münzer and others) were eliminated. Today, partially under the influence of the Marxist critique of the Reformation, many Christian interpreters have begun to think that the left-wing Reformers were more responsible toward the oppressed elements of their society than were the central Reformers, whose interests became too closely bound to those of the ruling classes.

Finally, let us look at an example out of the present situation of the church under the cross today. In East Germany, the church at its best (as in a figure like Johannes Hamel of Naumburg) gives what I would call a prophetic image of the role of the Christian community in relation to government. There, the church has been driven out of the ruler's house. It has had to live by its wits. This has been hard for a church which previously had been supported by the government to an inordinate degree. But because it is no longer tied to the government, it is able to be prophetically critical of the state, while at the same time giving every indication of its support for the truly human policies and programs of the Marxist-Leninist ideal. Just because it has not been able to claim "rights," it is possible for this church to engage in a remarkably honest appraisal of what is good and what is questionable in the state. It cannot do this easily, or without suffering. But Christ never promised his church freedom from suffering.

The rule for the prophetic community in relation to power—if now we may generalize on the basis of these illustrations—is this: the prophetic church does not represent *itself,* its needs, desires, or rights; rather, as it stands before those in authority, it represents "the neighbor." More particularly, it represents the elements of the society who are hungry, imprisoned, naked, oppressed. *The essence of the prophetic community in relation to power is its vigilance for humanity.*

From Organizer to Participant

Christianity not only lives in this world alongside government; it also lives with other organizations, groups, and movements. With some it has a good deal in common at the level of sociopolitical, economic, ethical, and cultural concern. How, in the new diaspora situation, might the church relate to these others?

Again we have to reflect first on the ways the church has tried to relate to such movements and causes in the past. Here there has been no single approach, but a variety of approaches. Some parts of the church universal have been more open to such movements and causes than have others. There have been admirable attempts, especially in the quite recent past, to work together with agencies and organizations whose causes Christians can identify themselves with: migrant workers, various racial groups, women, the gay community, the movement of protest against unjust war, etc.

And yet, when we have acknowledged these attempts, we have also to acknowledge that every one of them has been met by staunch opposition from within the church itself, as well as from established dimensions of the culture at large. While a protesting element in the church has made itself felt in our time in a new and even remarkable way, it is still only an element. This by itself is not so significant for our present analysis. What is significant, rather, is what the conventional church uses in its fight against its own protesting element. It uses the same old arguments and tactics that belong to the Constantinian model of the church.

What I mean, in concrete terms, is that in its relation to these other groups, the dominant wing of official Christianity operates very carefully and predictably within a certain set of rules: (1) The church can support movements and causes that are clearly within the realm of conventional Christian morality. (2) The church can support these other groups so long as its identification with them does not compromise the church (i.e., so long as fraternization with such groups does not get the church into trouble with its primary sponsor, the dominant culture, including government). (3) The church will take part in activities involving other groups provided it can maintain a clear organizational autonomy and (still more desirable) a clear-cut authority. It would in fact be better, according to this mentality, for the church itself to initiate any such mutual activities, so as not to become the victim of the manipulation of other groups. (This is what is meant by the term "organizer" in the heading of this section.)

The church will go thus far in relating to and supporting other movements and causes with which it can recognize some affinity of social or ethical aims. But there are definite points beyond which it will not venture. These points are nowhere stated in black and white, yet every churchgoer knows intuitively what they are. Certain groups and movements are almost wholly avoided by loyal churchmen and churchwomen. This varies somewhat, geographically and sociologically, but it is not purely relative. The Marxists represent for most Christians a dangerous group with which to associate, even when parallels between Marxism and Christianity are accepted at the theoretical level. We are happy to talk about liberation theology today and to be associated with some groups within our own society when blatant forms of oppression can be identified. But we will take this concern "only so far." The point where radical criticism threatens our own economic and political structures and the powers vested in them is too far.

It would be instructive in this context to speak about the gay rights movement and Christian response to it. It is so complex an issue that it cannot easily be used as an illustration. In one respect, it is a graphic example of the willingness to go "only so far" on the part even of liberal elements in the church. As for the conservative and dominant elements, they would return to the earlier ironclad isolationism of Christian ethical endeavor.

How can the church that is coming to be manifest a different spirit in relation to other groups, movements, and causes? Of course it must again be a matter of trial and error, experimentation, and corporate thought and planning. But I would make one suggestion, coming out of the preceding analysis: The beginning of a new attitude toward the other movements and humanitarian causes would have to grow out of a new theology! It is as basic as that. By a new theology I mean both a new approach to our faith as such and, in the more restrictive sense of the word "theology," a new understanding of the divine. Who is God? Is he *our* God only? Who is Jesus Christ? Is he captured in our Christology? Who is the Spirit? Do Christians have possession of him (or her)? Is God able to be only where we are, to work only where we work? Are we self-announced Christians the only ones who obey him and carry him into the dark places of human existence?

Whoever pays close attention to the Bible at this point knows that the answers to all these questions must be a resounding "No!" God is infinitely greater than our conceptions of him, and he is more pervasively at work in the world than our theologies can ever grasp. God is infinitely more than merely God, as Martin Buber has said.

The "God beyond God" (Tillich) is present and active in his beloved world. Paul Lehmann expresses it in a phrase that I greatly admire: God is at work in the world "to make and to keep human life human" (*Ethics in a Christian Context,* see especially Chapter III, pp. 74ff.; Harper & Row, 1963). He himself is at work. We do not initiate this work, he does. He establishes his humanizing, liberating work in unpredictable ways, among unlikely people. He uses all kinds of strange combinations of human energy, emotion, and motivation. The only thing that is predictable about the God of the Bible is that whatever he does is determined by his love for his creation, especially for its articulate center, the human race. Beyond that, nothing is predictable. The "good shepherd" can be recognized only because he has the welfare of the sheep at heart. The "shepherd" may appear in odd disguises. One day he may be a policeman and the next day a student protesting police oppression. He may be a Christian statesman moving in high and dangerous places, or an atheist philosopher tempting naïve students away from their superficial Sunday school religion. He may be black, he may be white. He may be religious or secular. He may be straight or gay. He may be she. There is no telling, because the ways of the loving God are as mysterious, and finally as logical, as the needs of the human race. The only thing one can go by is the intuition of the spirit of love—of suffering love, of *agapē.* Where love is, there

is God. Where human life is being "kept"—enhanced,
preserved, liberated—there is God.

The business of the Christian community is not to
organize God's work for him, but to participate in it
wherever it finds that work in progress.

The church that listens for the voice of this Good
Shepherd will inevitably find itself in strange places,
with strange people. Camillo Torres knew what that
meant. Though he himself was not a Marxist, he knew
that he had to go more than the second mile with the
Marxists. In the long run, he had to go almost all the
way. There is no guarantee of safety. There is no guarantee, either, that one's Christian confidence will keep
one from being confused, even lost. One will wonder
whether whatever faith one had is lost. Many people,
working among various liberating groups and movements in different parts of the world, wonder: Am I still
a Christian? Have I lost that perspective? Such questions come to the Christian whenever he or she
becomes deeply involved in the human struggle. It happened to Dietrich Bonhoeffer. It is perhaps what happens, profoundly, to all those whom we call "saints." To
be the friend of humanity is sometimes to wonder if
God is not the enemy. At least it means to know the
temptation of thinking that he has abandoned us. One
has to come that close to Golgotha. This is part of "living
on the boundary."

But there is something undeniably authentic in this
temptation, if we keep in mind the one we acknowledge as our Lord. He became so involved with human
life and the cause of human destiny that he found himself, at last, aligned with all the wrong people, against
the people who defined for his society such matters as

morality, decorum, and religion. Between the two criminals, and prior to that in the Garden of his agony, he must have wondered whether he had not gone too far. Too far into the darkness. I suspect that being a Christian in the church of the future will usually mean living with that kind of temptation. Most of the Christians I know in churches of Eastern Europe live with the temptation that they may have sold out to Marxism. There are always people around them, and voices from Western Christendom, who taunt them with being traitors to the Christ. But this is part of what it means to live under the cross, to suffer with the crucified One. It is part of the suffering that is the mark of the true church. If Christians, as a community or as individuals, have no *trouble* thinking themselves Christian, then there may be something quite questionable in the form of Christianity that has been assumed. "Therefore let any one who thinks that he stands take heed lest he fall" (I Cor. 10:12).

From Purveyor of Exclusive Truth
to Partner in the Search

The final area of relationship between church and world is the relationship of Christianity and the other religions of the world. This area of concern is so complex that it requires far more attention than can be devoted to it here. However, it cannot be overlooked in this discussion. Perhaps in this area the real character of the new diaspora church is most clearly revealed. In both of the previous areas of relationship, we have been thinking more or less about external matters, ethical as distinct from theological problems, though the two are not really separable. Here we have to think about theology. Indeed we have to go to the heart of our belief. We cannot ask how Christianity relates to the other religions of mankind without raising questions of content. Is Christian truth absolute, ultimate, final? If the answer is affirmative, then it follows that the church's relation to the other religions of the world will reflect this. Is Christian truth merely one version of reality among others? This belief will lead to a quite different answer to the question, How should Christianity relate to the other world religions? In short, here we have to do with *what is believed,* not only with the way we conduct ourselves as believers.

There is little doubt about the way we have been in the past. With some notable exceptions, Christianity has put itself forward in the world as the purveyor of exclusive and final religious truth. In the times of its greatest power, moreover, the church did not stop with *religious* truth in pressing its claims to ultimacy. It regarded itself as having the edge on all truth. Truth is after all "of God," and the church is the representative of God on earth. Therefore the church is the receiver and preserver of divine truth. Thus went the rationale for the thought control and persecution, not only of those who differed religiously, but of any who brought forward any sort of truth claim which seemed to call in question the Christian version of reality. It is not necessary to give examples; they are all too well remembered. One name—Galileo—serves to conjure up the whole long list.

Modern Christianity has managed, at last, to get over the worst aspects of this exclusivism. There are still many confessed Christians who deny any sort of scientific truth which clashes with their interpretation of the Scriptures. But on the whole we have become more modest about matters of natural and applied sciences.

When it comes to *religious* truth, however, we are still terribly immodest. For the most part we are at one with the perpetrators of the Inquisition. Though we are too humane to execute the heretics of other religious persuasions, the same mentality informs our hearts: we know we are right! (I am speaking about the most representative Christianity in North America today.) This conviction lies behind our efforts in world mission. Everybody must know the truth, and we possess it. We are the truth's curators and teachers.

This mentality has colored in particular our attitude toward the Jews. That is partly because the Jews were for so many centuries the only "unbelievers" who could be found in any great numbers in the midst of Christendom. But at a deeper level our feeling of superiority to the Jews lies in our belief that the Jewish way, including the partial truth of the "Old Testament," had been superseded. The Messiah has come, and the Jews have rejected him. The Temple, the Law, the sacrificial system, the whole religion of Israel has been surpassed. There should be no more Jews. Still the continuing presence of the Jews right in the heart of Christendom has been a constant reminder to an imperialistic church that a people could reject the truth and yet live— maybe even prosper, as the Rothschilds and others did! Judaism thus constituted an affront to the Christian conviction that the church possesses ultimate truth. European Christianity could not rest content until the Jews had been refuted. It mattered little whether Judaism was refuted through conversion, or expulsion, or possibly more severe measures. The "final solution" to "the Jewish question" was not (thank God) undertaken by the Christians themselves; but centuries of Christian unrest over the Jews certainly contributed in a major way to the Nazi enterprise of extermination. After Auschwitz, the question about our relation to Judaism (and therefore to all other religious traditions as well) is no longer a merely theoretical question. It is a question of the most existential and painful sort.

As Rosemary Ruether and others have recently pointed out, we cannot face this question merely by developing new forms of charity. (Cf. Rosemary Ruether, *Faith and Fratricide: The Theological Roots of Anti-Semitism;* Seabury Press, 1974. A response to this important book on the part of various scholars has just appeared under the title *Anti-Semitism and the Foundations of Christianity;* Alan Davies, ed.; Paulist Press, 1979.) "Brotherhood Week" and the like will not suffice, for the problem is deeper. It is a problem of content— of theology. So long as Christians regard their version of religious truth as absolute and final, it will be necessary for them to consider the Jews and all the others as adhering to inferior versions of the truth, if not to downright error.

Is it, then, the destiny of the new diaspora church to follow the example of Christian liberalism? The liberal answer to the problem of the relation between Christianity and all the other religions was and is to say that they all have some share of the truth. A special version of this idea, held by many liberal Christian intellectuals, runs like this: In each of the great religions of mankind there are symbolic forms, concepts, and practices which seem to exclude each other so long as we stick in a literal way to these symbolic expressions. But if we try to get at the meaning behind the symbols, what we discover is that all the religions constitute different ways of expressing similar truths. Wise persons, therefore, will not take the particular symbols of their own religious tradition with ultimate seriousness; at least they will qualify the seriousness with which they regard them by setting them in the perspective of the deeper religious reality that they express. These persons may continue, in that case, to be Jewish, Muslim, or Christian, but they will know that they stand in a close relation with all the others, who express the same or similar truth in their own ways.

There is no doubt in my mind that this attitude is preferable to the old imperialism of conventional Christianity, with its triumphalistic pretensions. However, I am troubled by the liberal approach, too. I would not want to see it become the way out of this problem for the church of the future.

What troubles me about the liberal approach to other religions is this: I am not convinced that Christianity could forfeit its particularities, its particular "story," and come out at the same place. The liberal approach assumes that there is a purer, truer religious truth which stands behind all the particular "stories" of the religions. Is that in fact really so? It is typical of intellectual mentality, with its special kind of pride, to imagine that it can rise above particularities, above symbols and mythologies, to the place where naked, unmasked, abstract truth is found. In that case, why wouldn't anyone who took this attitude form a new religion: the religion of ultimate truth behind the symbols, abstract truth above the stories, demythologized truth beneath the myths of the religions? Indeed, that proposal, in a great many forms, has long since been put forward, and can still be found today. These purposively constructed religions always come out saying things that are in fact quite different from Biblical faith—or from any other historic religion. Usually what they achieve is the affirmation of the values and opinions of their formulators, reflecting quite naturally the values and opinions of the social contexts of those formulators: e.g., nineteenth-century United States (the Ethical Culture movement); twentieth-century South Korea (the Unification Church), or the British and American world of liberal intellectuals (various forms of Unitarianism, etc.). Thus both in its popular and its more sophisticated manifestations, the liberal attempt to create a positive relationship between the various religions ends, at the theoretical level, in a merger of all religious phenomena, in which the distinctiveness of each religion is sacrificed or considered penultimate. At the practical level, all that liberalism has achieved in this respect is the provision of a few more religious (and often purely sectarian) alternatives to an already saturated world.

What I would propose as an alternative to both the conventional and the liberal Christian ways of relating to other religions no doubt comes closer to the liberal alternative. But it would differ in at least one important respect. Instead of counseling my fellow Christians to *rise above* the "mythologies" of their faith, I would say that they should *go more deeply into them.* Don't try to explain away the particularities of your tradition. Don't try to exchange all your symbols for straightforward explanations. Don't give up your Story! Rather, enter into it more deeply.

Entering more deeply into the Christian story means many things. In a central way it means taking with utter seriousness the fact that it is a Story, not a bundle of doctrines. And it means taking even more seriously the fact that what stands at the center of this Story is not a moral, or an object lesson, or an abstract truth, or a principle of salvation but ... *a Person!* The Story cannot be reduced to theory. No story can! The Story at the center of Christian faith—by which I mean that long story of Israel and of the man of the cross who emerged out of that story and gave it, for Christians, a certain *denouement*—this Story is far more gripping, more elusive, more meaningful than are any of our theological and exegetical commentaries upon it. Nor is it ever to be equated with those commentaries. No one would think of substituting the commentary of a literary critic for the novel that he was commenting upon, or a Bach fugue for the dull explanations musicologists provide about it! Why then should we ever imagine that theology, or doctrine, or Biblical interpretation—or even, for that matter, the Bible itself—could be substituted for the Story. *Every* good story transcends its own articulations, and every *good* story has to be told again and again, always in different ways, in order to communicate its essence to the changing scene of humanity. The Story at the heart of the Christian message and Christian existence is no exception. It transcends *all* its expressions, even the Biblical one; and it is always more profound, in its essential simplicity, than all our attempts to articulate, explain, or contain it. It can speak for itself, very often, without our explanations—as all good stories can. It can find a hearing with many diverse groups of human beings, not because it is abstract and

general enough to transcend all human particularities,
but precisely because it is concrete and specific. As it
has been said frequently in our time, Christians have to
live with the gospel as a "scandal of particularity": this
particular people, this particular man, Jesus, this particular sequence of events. Always the question comes:
Why not some other people, some other man, some
other historical sequence? Why not Socrates? Gandhi?
Schweitzer?

But the other side of the *scandal* of particularity is
the *necessity* of particularity. The universal (universal
truth, universal love, etc.) comes to historical creatures
like ourselves only in the form of particular manifestations. I do not meet Woman, I meet this woman. I do
not encounter Love, I encounter the love of this person
here and now. The weakness of the liberal attempt to
rise above the particulars of the Christian Story (and
other Stories) is that in the last analysis it abstracts humanity from its historical context, which is always full
of particularities. No living beings can sufficiently overcome their own concrete humanity to be able to grasp
the universals that are offered them. And in reality all
the so-called universals derived by this liberal search for
truth above the particularities of religion are themselves only disguised particularities, reflecting quite historically conditioned values and goals, namely, the values and goals of those who construct these universalist
religious alternatives.

A deepened reflection on the character of "the Story"
provides us with a new point of departure in our consideration of other religions. What stands at the center of
the Story we tell is not a "what" at all, but a "who": a
Person. And preceding him there is a whole line of

quite concrete, historical persons (Israel), and after him comes another long line of persons (the church). And beyond them all a "heavenly" Person—the Eternal Thou, who is not in the least to be confused with an abstract principle of power or energy, as in the religion of the Deists.

When the New Testament puts this Person at the center of the Story, it tells us that the reality with whom we have to do, in faith, is concrete, accessible, and transcendent. Consider this: The New Testament does not provide us with naked truth, once for all articulated. It provides us rather with a living being who is one of us, and who says: "I *am* the truth." Jesus did not hand his disciples a book that contained all the right beliefs and morals. He didn't even dictate maxims or commandments or theories to them (most of them were illiterate anyway!). He did talk with them, and no doubt they remembered, more or less accurately, some of the things he said to them. While all of that is important, it isn't ultimately important. For the disciple community, not his teachings, but he himself, is what is ultimately important. What they remembered, mostly, was *him.* His teachings, which they more or less remembered, are important because they help us to get a picture of who *he* was. "The truth" is bound up with his very being: "I *am* the truth." You can experience this truth, but you cannot possess it. You cannot control it. You cannot even understand it. You are grasped by it, but you cannot yourself grasp it. You cannot possess the truth that Jesus "is" any more than you can possess your wife or your best friend. You just have to live with this truth—to be open to it, moment by moment. And that is precisely what *faith* is all about.

How does this affect our relationship with other beliefs, other religious traditions? It affects that relationship profoundly by providing us Christians with a new understanding *of ourselves,* especially of ourselves in relation to the question of truth. The *new* understanding is not really new, but it has hardly ever informed our life as a church in relation to other religious traditions. In our most characteristic encounters with them, we have pictured ourselves as the possessors of ultimate truth, final revelation. Going into any sort of human relationship with that self-image can produce only what it has in fact produced: arrogance in us, defensiveness in others.

What if the church began to understand that it really does not *possess* any truth? What if it began in earnest to think of itself as being possessed *by* a truth that forever eludes it? What if it began to realize—and not merely on occasion to mouth!—the fact that if *Jesus Christ* is "the truth," then its ideas and doctrines and theological explanations of him are *not?* What if the church, even at this eleventh hour, began to understand its own Bible, which never points to itself or says "I am the truth" but points to an incarnate Word transcending its words, a Voice transcending its commandments, a Spirit transcending its letter? What if the church began to comprehend what it means that we shall not make "graven images"; that the "daily bread" of the living God cannot be stored up; and that we shall have no other gods besides the One who is so ungraspable that even his Name is a mystery and a riddle? What if the church, in short, began to know that at the center of the Story it tells there is a Word incarnate, and a cross?

Would not this new comprehension provide an altogether different atmosphere for the relationship between the church and the others who seek after God? Would it not bring to the Christians in particular a certain modesty about themselves—ourselves? Modesty, not only as a moral quality, but *intellectual modesty?* We need the modesty principle, not as an ethical byproduct of Christian charity, but as a humility built into our faith and our theology. Brotherhood Week may draw upon ethical qualities of one kind and another. But only a revised understanding of who we are in relation to "the truth" can bring about the kind of modesty that is prerequisite to genuine dialogue. We have to know that we, too, are *searchers* after "the truth," and to lose every trace of the former arrogance of those who "possess" it.

The very confession of faith in Jesus Christ implies that, far from possessing the truth, we are only those who "hunger and thirst" for it. But while this necessity has always been built into our Story, it has until now been kept from informing our actual existence as church. Because the church has heretofore existed in the world as conquering and triumphalistic Christendom, it could not "hear" its own Story. Its Story put it in the ranks of those who hope for what they do not possess; its sociological reality made it conceive of itself as the possessor of everything hoped for. But this sociological situation has now changed radically. The diaspora church can therefore open itself in a new way to its own story. The result will be a different understanding of itself in relation to the other religious traditions of the human race.

This is the beginning of a new openness to the others.

It is not all that needs to be said, but it is the necessary point of departure for everything else. Without something like this, either Christianity will become ridiculous in its exclusivistic pretensions to truth or it will be absorbed into a general religiousness that no longer remembers the cross of the incarnate Word. Without that cross we have nothing to bring to the dialogue with the others. But if we continue to make that cross synonymous with our theories about it, there can be no dialogue at all. At this point, the theology of the cross means that we have to put to death our own claims to ultimate truth and let the cross of Golgotha establish what it really does establish: the solidarity of the loving God with anguished, searching humanity in all its many quests for salvation.

The Courage to Change

We stand at a difficult crossroads in the history of the Christian church. From our past, we have inherited ways of being with the others with whom we share life in this world; and these ways of being are called into question by the whole contemporary experience of humanity. The old, imperialistic church of the centuries cuts a silly figure in the world today when it tries to lord it over others, both at the level of thinking and at the level of doing. A Christianity which behaves in that superior way is absurd. It is like a figure of some bygone age, a Rip Van Winkle who comes into the contemporary scene thinking he can still conduct himself as he did in the old days. In many ways, contemporary Christianity is just such a Rip Van Winkle. It has been asleep. It hasn't noticed that the world, meantime, was able to get along without it, or that others have come along to take its place or at least to give it hearty competition—even for the little area of human life that the world leaves open to its "religions."

It is hard for us Christians, even when we know that our old, imperialistic way of behaving is passé; it is hard for us to open ourselves to the new mode of being to which I have tried to point in this discussion. I suspect that the churches will continue for a long time still to resort to the old habits when "dealing with" the state, various movements and causes in the world that parallel its concerns, and other religious traditions. But increasingly we will be brought to know that these ways of being are no longer possible or permitted. Some of us have already been able to admit, at the intellectual level at least, that these ways of being have never been either desirable or consistent with our own best traditions—our Story. Eventually, both by willing it and by being forced into it, more and more Christians will find the courage to change.

In the final chapters, we shall attempt to envisage what might come of that courage.

VI

PRACTICALLY SPEAKING

An Apology for Presumption

I must begin with an apology. It is presumptuous for a teacher of theology, working mostly within an academic institution, to say what he thinks will—or ought to—become the life-style of the church of the future. Pastors of congregations are in a better position to speak about that, if they will; so are informed lay persons.

However, as a teacher of prospective ministers I have a responsibility to follow through some of my more theoretical proposals, to ask what they would lead to in practice. I do not believe in the separation of theory and practice. Theology that is "pure theory" is no theology! Neither is practice without theological reflection good practice. If as a "theoretician" of Christian theology I am bold enough to speak about practice, I hope it will provoke some who are more deeply involved in ministry to exercise an equal boldness, and to attempt to bring a theological critique to bear upon their practice. There is no room for prima donnas in the church. Together, scholars and practitioners have to work through to a viable posture which the church can assume in these last decades of the twentieth century and beyond.

Another reason why I cannot avoid practical matters is that people in churches keep asking me: What, in practical terms, will the church of the future be like? I resist this question because too often it smacks of the old, predictable North American pragmatism. As a people, we find ourselves uncomfortable in the realm of ideas; we want to jump into the arena of action right away. Against this attitude I recall a saying I read one time on a church bulletin board: "Don't just do something, *sit there!*" Perhaps the most *practical* thing that most Christians could do at this time would be to "sit there," to begin to think, to reflect, to read, to meditate. We have not been a thoughtful church. We are naïve and lacking in self-knowledge. We tend to identify the problems we experience in church and society in simplistic ways. We shall have to become better thinkers if we want to become more relevant doers.

While I have resisted the temptation to speak practically and propose a program of action, it may be useful to try to envisage where some of these ideas would lead if they were put into practice. Such an attempt would at least help to make the theoretical analysis more concrete and graphic.

Besides, there are groups of earnest Christians on this continent today who are trying in all sincerity to envisage what shape the church of the future ought to assume. They are not attempting to avoid the deeper theoretical questions. They *are* open to painful theological reflection—a type of reflection the church has never encouraged in its laity. But at the same time they are confronted by practical questions of day-to-day existence of congregations. The congregation of which I am a member is an illustration: Sunday school enrollment is failing; attendance at church services is increasingly sparse, with elderly people predominating; financial crises loom on the immediate horizon. I have enormous respect for the dedicated minister and the lay persons of this congregation, who have to face the practical questions. They must decide how we can continue, or whether we should; they must find new leadership in what seems a barren field. Because of my respect for these people, and the many others like them, I have tried to think about the most practical implications of the account that I have been giving of the church in these last days of the Constantinian era.

There is no one pattern for the present and future. Of that at least I am convinced. The diaspora church will work out its style of being in the world in different ways in different places. In other words, the form of the church will be determined by situational or contextual considerations. What is suitable here will not be suitable or desirable there. The particularities of the situation must shape the church, with tradition and the ecumenical church offering what guidance they can.

What follows, then, is not a program for everyone to follow. It should be understood as illustrative of a way —*one* way—of working out some of the issues that confront the church in our time. In reality, what will happen in the churches is already happening. We are in a period of transition and a great variety of things are being tried. Some of our ideas will work, others will be found premature or foolish. We have to be open to experimentation and to variety. We have to trust that what is good will prosper—provided we remember that to speak of prospering, according to the logic of the cross, is not a way of speaking about worldly success.

The Basics

Having offered these reservations, I turn to the task at hand: a scenario of the church of the future—tomorrow's Christian diaspora, which here and there is already manifesting itself. What are the basics in this scenario?

I believe that all—or most—of the things I have said in the foregoing chapters are basic to the church that is coming to be: That it is a diaspora, not Christendom reconstructed; that it is movement, not institution; that it lives on the boundary between its own traditional expression and the contemporary world; that it is neither ghetto nor cultural religion; that it seeks to relate to the work that God is doing in the world, wherever it may happen upon that work. All of these things seem to me basic. But instead of simply summarizing all these points, I want to distill from them some fundamental generalizations, and then move on to the practical implications of these generalizations. What, then, does it all boil down to? I would answer that it comes down to two rudimentary theses, two "musts."

First: *The church that is coming to be must be possessed by a new awareness of the uniqueness of the Christian message and way.*

Second: *The church's life must be determined by an overwhelming sense of commitment to the world, not in terms of dominance, but in terms of service.*

The first thesis—that the church must have a new

awareness of the uniqueness of the Christian message and way—could easily be misunderstood. It *would* be misunderstood if anyone took the word "uniqueness" as a synonym for "superiority." Whether the Christian message and way are *superior* to other messages and other ways is a matter for every human being to decide, and ultimately for God to decide. It is not our business to recommend Christianity on such grounds. But it is our business to find out what is *unique* about this Christian Story—why it is different; why it should not be absorbed into a general religious perspective; why it should be preserved as a statement about God and man and their relationship. We should find out simply *what it is!* If the church cannot do this, it has no business perpetuating the Christian gospel at all. At this point in history, nothing will keep the Christian faith going automatically. It stands or falls on the merits of its own account of the human condition. It is our task to find out what these "merits" are—to learn for ourselves what our tradition has been, what story has been told, and how it might be retold in our time.

In the past, it was not necessary for Christians to do that. Certainly not for ordinary members of congregations and parishes. Well, not even for most clergy! Some scholars in every age worked on these basic questions. They worked their way through the faith again in an original way, bringing to it the questions of their own place and time. But they were always a small minority of the Christians. Most of the baptized, lay and clerical, had no such necessity placed upon them. Christianity could be preserved as a matter of course, for it was part of the structure of the society itself.

But now—and even more in the immediate future—

it will be the task of everybody to become theologians.
Not only the scholars, not only the clergy, but every
Christian will have to undertake the difficult business of
trying to understand what is believed. That task alone
will provide a sufficient reason for remaining in the
church. Those who are not able to "give a reason for the
hope that is in them" will not bother staying. There will
be no fringe benefits—there aren't any even now! We
only remain in the church because it makes some sense
to us—this message, this way. Moreover, *we have to
continue to discover for ourselves the sense that it
makes.* It isn't enough to have discovered it once, to
have experienced a "conversion." The only real conver-
sions are continuing experiences. We remain in the
church, in spite of the inevitable dry periods of faith and
the continuing temptation to give it all up, because we
are able to discover something that keeps us with it. We
get a perspective on existence from this Story that we
can't get elsewhere. As the disciples said to Jesus when
he asked them if they, too, were going to leave him:
"Lord, to whom shall we go? You have the words of
eternal life" (John 6:68).

The second thesis—that the church must have a deep
commitment to the world, a commitment to serve—is,
of course, closely related to the first. If you like, it is the
"horizontal dimension," whereas the first was the "ver-
tical dimension." A church that really continues to open
itself to the understanding of its own gospel will be
driven by what it understands into the world for which
that gospel is meant. As the gospel is the Story of the
incarnation of God's Word, the bearers of the gospel
must themselves become incarnate in the life of the
world.

Sometimes I think that the church has never understood that, not even in its early days. Though some individuals certainly grasped it, what prevented the earliest Christian communities from following through was their expectation of the early *end* of the world. They could become a community of prayer and withdrawal from the world because they thought the whole creational experiment would soon be terminated. They went to the world with their gospel, to be sure, but mostly in order to snatch people out of the world before it was too late. They set out to save those who could be saved—as brands from the burning. Then, after Christianity became the established religion in the fourth century, it was too busy dominating the world to think of serving the world.

One thing is quite exciting about the present prospects of the church. Perhaps for the first time in history, the church can be open to something that is central to its own gospel: the service of the human family and its environment. There will always be sects that wait for the Second Coming and find in that expectation a sufficient reason for being. And there will likely always be groups in the church that claim absolute authority in the world. But neither of these historical postures is any longer viable for the church. Either we will embrace the image of the church as servant, or we will have no reason to continue in it. I am stating this not only as a unique possibility that is open to us today but also as a necessity that has been laid upon us.

History has prepared the way for such a community. There are many groups and many individuals in today's world who know that the human race, if it is to survive, can only survive "together." Earth's creatures are ecologically and spiritually intertwined. Who can provide anything like enthusiastic motivation and direction of the kind that is needed to inspire programs of survival, conservation, limitation of greed, feeling for the totality, feeling for the neighbor and the oppressed? Not alone, in isolated grandeur and saintliness, but humbly and in company with all the others who may be found, a Christian community that has explored the depths of its own "unique gospel" (our first thesis) can become an intelligent and inspired servant of humanity in such a world as this. A rare bird indeed!

If the two theses with which we began represent the basic necessities, they contain in turn certain practical implications for the life of the church that manifests them. The implications are of course boundless. But some expression of them will provide a further elaboration of the model of the church we are attempting to develop.

An Emphasis on Learning

An immediate implication of the first thesis is *a strong emphasis on learning.* If there is to be any real appreciation for the uniqueness of the Christian message and way, then many persons within the church will have to become students of the Christian tradition in a way that this has never occurred in the past. Naturally it does not mean that everyone must become a professional theologian! I believe there will always be a place in the Christian community for intensive and specialized scholarship of many kinds. It will always be necessary for a few in the community to become theologians and historians, Biblical interpreters and interpreters of the times in the more rigorous sense. But the division between ordinary Christians and educated Christians that has pertained in all the centuries past is no longer workable in the diaspora situation. No one legislates this division out of existence; it simply passes away, because those who cannot or will not devote themselves to study and understanding will lack the inner motivation to remain in the Christian church. This is not a process reserved for the future; it is already occurring, and it has been occurring for several generations.

Within the general category of learning there are many side issues to be considered. One is the *education of the young.* Part of the reason for the decline of the Sunday school, especially in recent years, is that our attempts to educate the young have seldom been backed up with serious adult education in the congregation. How can we expect the children to study the faith in earnest when they are surrounded by adults who apparently aren't the least interested in studying? It is comparable to parents who expect their children to read books, when all the parents do is look at television! The need to study, to learn, to understand, must inform *the whole community* of faith. Learning will not succeed if it applies only to the young.

Indeed, insofar as the young in the church are concerned, the diaspora church would know perfectly well that it cannot depend upon its own young to replenish its ranks. The child of Christian parents, in the diaspora situation, is not expected to become a Christian as a matter of course. There is no intrinsic reason why my son should be a Christian. I fervently hope that he will at least find something significant in this faith. If he judges it a vain superstition, that would be a judgment on his parents, too; and one does not wish for that. But I cannot *assume* that he will respect Christian faith—let alone that he will become a Christian himself. Obviously the serious Christian community will want to give its children and youth the most carefully thought out introduction to Christian faith that is possible for them. It will not substitute "coloring" for the Bible, or little lessons in bourgeois morality and "values" for difficult lessons in the meaning of the Trinity. That kind of accommodation belongs to the Constantinian situation, where it could be assumed that Junior would follow Senior into the flock of Christ. The effort to educate the young must be more rigorous in the diaspora situation. But for all its rigor, it will never be able to presume that children will graduate from their junior schools of theology into church membership as if no leap of faith, no repentance, no struggle were involved.

In what has come to be called "Christian education," Christians could again learn much from the living community of Israel. Israel has always known the importance of learning. Every *historical* faith—every religion that assumes a *revelational* basis—has to stress the importance of learning. One is not born with historical knowledge; one has to acquire such knowledge. Moreover, it is not easy to acquire a profound knowledge of events that occurred centuries ago. Yet without some real knowledge of these events, the whole Christian enterprise is reduced to subjectivity and sentimentality. *That* is what happened to our Sunday schools.

Under the impact of modern, child-centered education, and in reaction against the old orthodox cramming of catechetical information, educators set aside the subject matter of the faith in favor of exploring the child's own world, its inner life. In doing this—the evils of which are now being recognized more outside than inside the church—Christianity forfeited its historical, revelational character.

Even worship, when it can no longer presuppose an educated awareness of the foundational events of the faith, becomes inconsequential and frequently meaningless. When Jesus says, "Do this in remembrance of me," he has in mind something more mysterious than a *mere* historical acquaintance with the events surrounding his life. Nevertheless, without that historical knowledge and some rational reflection upon its meaning, there can be no deeper, liturgical "remembering" either. Without a studied meditation on the primary events of the "history of salvation," faith degenerates into a superficial kind of mysticism.

Israel has *always* known this. Its holy book, the commentaries on that book, the ongoing life of study, the respect in which learning is held even by nonreligious Jews—this is testimony to the fact. But in the diaspora situation (which Israel had to occupy throughout the Christian era, and before), education becomes even more important. Because the community of faith can no longer count on external things to keep itself alive, it has to learn to live by remembering its own tradition. It learns its Story always afresh, always in the context of a culture indifferent or hostile to the Story, always in the presence of powerful alternative world views. If Israel has been a *living* tradition in a way that the church has not (and I believe this to be so), it is because Israel could not take its continuation for granted or depend on the state or the culture or the atmosphere to perpetuate its tradition. Each congregation, each family, each father and mother had to become "teacher"—and over against the kind of worldly opposition we Christians know nothing about. But we shall have to learn about that opposition in the years to come. And we shall have to become a community of teachers, like Israel, if we want to survive at all.

To carry this emphasis on learning a step farther: I can discover no more appropriate paradigm for the Christian community of the diaspora church than the one that is given in the Jewish experience: *the synagogue.* I am naturally not suggesting that every Jewish synagogue actually achieves this purpose; but the idea is the right one. I would insist that *the normal form of the coming church's corporate life would be the form of the synagogue*—or, as we may call it, *the house of study.* Formed around such a concept, the congregation would neglect neither worship on the one hand nor service in the world on the other. But the primary and integrating emphasis of the ongoing daily and weekly life of the *koinōnia* would be its study.

By study I am not referring to a purely intellectual activity. Certainly I do not mean the passionless sort of study that is advocated by the contemporary educational system. I mean the sort of existentially involved study characteristic of, e.g., the Hasidic communities of Israel, or some monastic communities, or even Marxist communes. The character of *what* is studied must always determine the mode and method of study. If what is studied by the Christians is really the rudiments of their own faith and their position in the world, there would be no danger of study becoming a merely intellectualistic or arid pursuit!

Perhaps the house of study could be located in a

building (some of the less pretentious churches of today could be utilized for this purpose). On the other hand it might meet in people's houses, as in the so-called house-church movement. The physical circumstances are not *very* important. What is important is the symbol and the reality of concentrated, scholarly, involved engagement with the faith in the context of our life in this world.

It is not hard to foresee the criticism of such an idea. It seems to turn the church into a university. Some of the Unitarians attempted something similar, didn't they? What a predictable thing for an academic to propose! Professors try to mold the whole church around their own little lives! Well, be assured that I have no interest in a church that mimics the university—especially not the contemporary university. It is hardly a viable paradigm for a community that seeks a certain unity of dialogue and understanding, the service of the greater human community, and the overcoming of the gap between subjectivity and objectivity. You have only to live in a modern university for a few years to know how improbable a model it is for what I have been advocating.

The "house of study" concept, or something comparable, must be built into our thinking and planning for the church of the future or we shall not have moved beyond the Constantinian church. If we imagine that a responsible Christian community is going to continue in the world without becoming a community of disciplined learning and interpretation, we are still living in another era. The transition of Christianity from institution to movement, from "Christendom" to diaspora, means that learning has to become central to the church's life as it has *never* done before. Only those who are able to articulate their belief with all the intelligence they can muster will withstand the winnowing process that is now being applied to Christianity. Christians must become at least as intelligent about their faith as the Marxists or the "Moonies" are about theirs, and it is hoped a little more modest in the bargain!

Functioning as a Priestly Community

From the second of our two basic theses (the necessity of a deep commitment to the world) I would draw what may be regarded by some as a surprising implication, namely, *that the church must understand itself and function as a priestly community.* I would associate the priestly life of the Christian community with its sense of commitment *to the world.* If that commitment is really the context of the church's priestly activity (including its worship), it will help to prevent the sin that has plagued it from the outset: its tendency to *segregate* the church from the world. But here elaboration is needed.

The very mention of the word "priestly" may astonish certain Protestant readers. I want to assure them that I do not use this word lightly or easily. It can only be used, in fact, if it is radically reinterpreted. A good deal of what I feel to be wrong with the church lies precisely in a misleading appropriation of the concept of the priest and the priestly (i.e., holy) community.

Catholic use of the concept and Protestant avoidance of it is not the issue. The plain fact is that, by one means or another, Christians have used this concept of "priestliness" or "holiness," not in the *service* of the world but in their own service! Concretely, they have used it to distinguish themselves from the world, to keep for themselves a realm of authority and power in the world, and to sustain different sorts of hierarchical views of the status of human beings before the divine. The concept has meant a questionable kind of service: the service of a "chaplaincy" that blesses the world's projects, its banquets, its wars, its heroes, its space programs. On the one hand, the "priest" shows up in the world as religious authority; on the other hand, the "priest" appears as sycophant, bootlicker of those in power.

Against this actual performance of the Christian "priest," it is necessary to return to the roots of the Biblical concept of a priestly people. The basic meaning of priesthood is contained in the idea of *representation.* The priestly community (and priestliness belongs first to the *community* of the faithful, not to individuals or segments within it) functions in the world in a representative way. Its representation is twofold, as representation usually is. For example, the member of a governing body in democratic societies, on the one hand, represents his or her constituency in the parliament or congress and, on the other hand, represents *to* that constituency the decisions and aims of government. The concept of representation should not be confused with substitution. They are similar concepts, but, unlike the substitute, the representative acts "in *behalf* of" and not merely "instead of."

The priestly community of faith is called, on the one hand, to represent "the Christ" to and in the world. To grasp what that means, a great deal of rethinking of the meaning of "the Christ" is needed. For one thing, a church that thought of the Christ in terms of power and authority could imagine itself as rightly representing him when it dealt with people in high-handed ways. But Christ as he is actually given to us in the life of Jesus is not at all such a being. He is the crucified, the despised and rejected, the forsaken. To represent *such* a Christ does not mean to show up on the human scene as if one were a Caesar or a Napoleon. It may even mean to show up as the fool (Don Quixote), the poor man (Francis), the "idiot" (Dostoevsky), or the loser (Graham Greene's drunken priest). In short it will always mean to be sharply distinguished from what the world thinks of as authority, power, and glory. To represent "the Christ" in the form of worldly power and authority is to turn Jesus into the sort of messiah he resisted becoming in his wilderness temptations.

On the other hand, the Christian community is called to represent humanity—the world—before God. It is this aspect of the representational life of the people of God that has usually been ignored by historical Christianity. But it lies at the very core of the Biblical concept of priesthood and all its related concepts (election, holiness, sacrifice, vicarious suffering, etc.). To be the priestly community means not only to represent the crucified Christ in and to the world; it means to represent crucified *humanity* to God. It means to enter consciously and sincerely into the human quest for and struggle with God. It means to plead humanity's cause before God. Jesus in the Garden of Gethsemane is not just speaking for himself; he speaks as our "High Priest." And precisely as such it becomes his destiny to *struggle* with God. He does not lightly bow to the divine will; he resists, and passionately so. He must, because he is there before God in our behalf. As our representative he seeks an alternative to the way of the cross. Like Jacob/Israel struggling with the angel at the brook, Jesus our Priest insists that God should bless us in our own, human terms—meet our needs in our own way, answer our questions with answers we can understand and accept!

In the line of Jacob/Israel and of Jesus our High Priest, the church is called to assume also *this* side of the representative existence. In solidarity with broken, proud, anxious humanity, it is called to stand before God as the bearer of mankind's anxious and angry demands: "Why? What is the purpose of all this bloodshed, this hunger, this sickness and death? Is there any purpose, indeed? Can any of it be justified—can life itself be justified if even one child must suffer? Why don't you bless us? Why don't you redeem us—not only in theory, but in reality? What are you waiting for? Are you asleep? Have you absented yourself from the earth altogether, like an absentee landlord? Or are you perhaps ... dead? Or are you simply nonexistent, as the philosophers have been saying for a long time?"

The Psalms of Israel prominently include just this kind of wrestling with God. So does The Book of Job; so does most of the literature of Israel. There has been very little like it in the whole of Christianity. That is partly because we have substituted a Greek concept of God for the Hebraic one of the Scriptures. It is also partly because we in the Constantinian church have wanted to play the role of the intimates of God, possessing something of his power, majesty, and glory. We were so eager to be God's friends that we could not become the friend of people. Thus our failure to be a priestly community in the Bible's own terms stems directly from a failure to grasp the nature of the God with whom we have to do. For this God—the One who is so committed to humankind that he relinquishes his own glory and majesty and power in order to be "with us" —we substituted a god who retains every ounce of his awful dignity. Only such a god could serve the purposes of an official religion.

The "struggle with God" that is part of the church's priestly calling and living is an essential aspect of the kind of Christian *worship* that should be developed, I believe, in the diaspora church. I shall presently discuss that more fully. The purpose of introducing this dimension of the representative nature of the church at this point is that it is a necessary presupposition for *service in the world.* The service which Christ's church is called to perform in the world is not that of the Lady Bountiful, appearing to poor humanity with her basket full of goodies. It is that of the priest who can be priest only because all extraordinary "goodies" have been surrendered. The priest is made continually to stand solidly with those whom he or she represents. The representative can only *serve* humanity while participating in the life of humanity. If this is understood, it produces quite a different idea of service from the one that has prevailed in most forms of Christianity heretofore, though there have been notable exceptions. It has been difficult to inculcate such a concept of service in the dominant forms of Christianity because service based on solidarity with humankind simply did not fit the picture of Constantinian Christianity. In the diaspora church, however, it may be possible—in a new way— to recover something of the Biblical perspective on this question.

Practically speaking, for a church to have been grasped by that perspective on its priestly life would mean at least two things. First, the Christian community would not appear in the world with its agenda already in hand, its ethical program all worked out, its proposals for social change predetermined. Rather, it would learn gradually, through the suffering of an ongoing immersion in human life, what the problems were, what solutions were being attempted, what failures were experienced, what kind of proximate relief might be brought, what things would have to be borne in patience. It would mean losing our answers in favor of finding the real questions. It would not try to solve the world's problems so much as help to identify, clearly, what the problems are. To do this is no simple matter, especially in a society that looks always for the easiest statement of the problem in order to get on with the quickest solution. The church that attempted to apply something of "the wisdom of the cross" to the human community with which it stood in solidarity, would serve in a special way. It would help to separate superficial problems and false solutions, which are so characteristically substituted for the deeper issues—partly because entrenched and vested economic interests find it to their advantage to keep the problems, and the answers, simple! Together with all persons and agencies of goodwill, such a Christian community would help to isolate the great problems, to change what can be changed, to keep hope from giving way to fatalism and despair, and to evoke the courage to live with problems that defy ultimate solution.

Second, the diaspora church as priestly community would not *initiate* social change so much as identify the places where social change was already occurring. It would then work with those who were already struggling to bring about that change. As we observed earlier, God is not silent; he has other hands than Christian hands. He works constantly in the world "to make and to keep human life human" (Paul Lehmann). To be sure, he works in strange ways, with hands and voices and pens alien to *our* Way. But precisely what is needed in today's world, more than another "agent of social change" with its own program, competing with all the others, is a movement that can be perceived by all the others as having no vested interests. This would mean having no interest in propagandizing or proselytizing, no interest in becoming more popular with the masses, no interest in making gains for its own financial or numerical strength. It would mean a movement, in short, whose only motivation is solidarity and service. Only such a movement can be perceived by the others as a *forum* and a *catalyst*—a community which can here and there instill a little *mutual* trust between competing groups and causes. So many of the organizations with which Christians can make common cause, while having the interests of humanity at heart, can never quite escape the pride and aggressiveness of championing their own particular causes. The church knows well that method of operating in the world. To be perceived as a community without vested interests the church would have to give extraordinary signs of a change of heart! But if it does that, it has within its own tradition and self-understanding a potential for the kind of spontaneous service to others that is extremely rare in the world, if not unique.

It is not merely a theory or a dream that I am describing. Here and there, the churches have already begun to recognize the ubiquity of God's working in the world. It can be seen in organizations like Amnesty International, in the women's movement, in the quest for social, economic, and racial justice, in movements seeking to preserve the earth's resources for the future and distribute them equitably in the present. Here and there it has already happened that the *fruits* of a new, implicit self-image of the church have shown through. What is most needed now is a better theological understanding of this reality. Without such understanding, based on profound theological and critical reflection, the "fruits" of such a church can only occur as an intuitive response on the part of a few. And the few in whom this response comes forth will not understand what they are doing.

Scholars and teachers of the Christian church today must provide a model of the church and a theological rationale for this kind of social and ethical activity. It is not enough for the theologians of Christianity to say that they approve of Christians who engage in the struggles of migrant workers, or boycott fruit from South Africa, or oppose North American support of oppressive regimes in South America. The theological servants of the Christian community must interpret, both for those who are so engaged and for those who hesitate or who oppose such engagement, how that kind of solidarity belongs to our best heritage; how it is the logic of our belief itself; how it is the necessity which is laid upon us by divine providence, especially at this time, when life in the world is so fragile.

The Internal Life of Worship and Ministry

The final implication of our two basic theses has to do with the *internal life of the koinōnia*, in particular its *worship*, its *sacramental life*, and its *ministry*. We have suggested that if the uniqueness of the Christian message and way is to be preserved, the Christian community must become in a normative manner a house of study. We have further asserted that a church passionately committed to the world will function in it as a priestly community, representing the crucified Christ before humanity, and crucified humanity before its Lord.

This third implication belongs to both of the basic theses. It is, in a way, the place where they converge. The life of study and the life of priestly stewardship meet in the internal life of Christian congregations, in their worship and their ministry.

The internal life of the congregation is basic to the whole existence of the church. It should not be thought "a third consideration" just because it is treated in third place. All three of these implications are fundamental, to my mind; they belong together. The ancient quarrel between those who say that the church exists only for mission and those who claim the church exists only for its own sake is a false quarrel. Obviously the church does not exist for its own sake; it is a means to a greater end. The greater end is sometimes called "the Kingdom," and the church as it is described in the New Testament is not to be equated with the Kingdom of God. It is by no means certain that those who are sure they are the church even belong to God's Kingdom, or will ever make it. Others who do not even know the word "church" may be "first" in the Kingdom.

At the same time, while the *raison d'être* of the church is so much greater than itself in every way, the church is not *simply* a means. What is happening already within it, in a beginning sort of way and with much ambiguity, is an anticipation of God's Kingdom. It must be so, for otherwise the church would not be able to *be* a means to this greater end, or a symbol of its meaning. Even to become a means it must be something—it cannot be nothing, a mere formlessness, with neither content nor order. The church has continually to be formed and re-formed by its own message and the prophetic elements within it. Daily it must be judged, corrected, reshaped by the divine Spirit. Each morning it must be conformed anew to the love of God. It has always to become what it is—and to be rescued from the nothingness that it is always threatening to become.

Those who know me may express surprise that I make this strong claim for the internal life of the Christian community. For I am by no means a consistent or enthusiastic churchman. I find church services mostly uninspiring, often boring, sometimes maddening. I have a continuing quarrel with the structures of authority in churches. I find "the ministry" unusually entrenched, unimaginative, and bound to the status quo. The courts of the church are frequently preoccupied with trivia and so clergy-dominated that lay persons, in whom I have the greatest hope today, are discouraged from participation or numbed by the irrelevance of most of what transpires. But—for all that—I believe most sincerely in the importance of the internal life of the Christian community. Without it there could be no space for devoted study of the tradition or service in the world. Indeed, if I am sometimes at loggerheads with what I find by way of an internal life in the churches, it is because I have such a high concept of what might and what ought to be. As is usually the case with critics, my criticism originates in "great expectations." I am aware that the church of Jesus Christ is a community of sinners. I am not surprised at sin either trivial or heinous when I find it in the church. But *Christian* realism includes a strong component of hope, and in this sense it is highly *realistic* today to expect the Christian church to be something different from what it has been, for the most part, in the past. Paul Ehrlich, the ecologist, said that the world has become so fragile a place that the only realists around are those whom the "practical people" call idealists. If we cannot expect radical change in the Christian church (an institution that claims to be always reforming itself), how can we expect radical changes in the life-style of Western people in general? I would rather be a realist who thinks that human beings, confronted by extinction of one sort or another, will find the courage to change their ways, than the cynical sort of realist (often hidden beneath a self-styled liberalism and optimism) who says: Let it go to pot! Confronted by our particular form of extinction, Christianity *may* in this latter day become more nearly the church. This has been my theme from the outset of our study. If we accept this invitation, the church will have a future—perhaps even a great one (though not in the manner of its former "greatness"). If we do not accept it, what we call church will disappear—periodic swells of "evangelism," "spirituality," and revivalism notwithstanding. I do not think that the disappearance of what we call the church would mean the defeat of the God of the gospel. If his disciples were silent, said Jesus, the very stones would cry out. Nevertheless, I do not feel quite ready yet to leave it to the stones. Perhaps what follows should be entitled: "On Not Leaving It to the Stones"!

Worship

The first aspect of the internal life of the Christian community we should consider here is its worship. What is wrong with most of our existing worship is that it is unreal. I hesitate (as my teen-age children would not) to call it "phony." When it isn't just a matter of going through the motions, what we do is so unlike anything else that we do in this world that it comes over to honest persons as funny, quaint, or charming. Worship often devolves into pure sentimentality in the less liturgical denominations. In the traditionally liturgical churches one often finds pathetic attempts to be informal, with a new kind of formalization involving guitars, religious country-and-western music, and priests who dress in pastels. There are of course glorious exceptions to these generalizations. I am pointing to the fact that the changes we have been trying to make in worship are mostly trivial. The same old content comes through it all. For the tastes of a former, more aristocratic age we substitute the tastes of the middle class. We tear out the gilded bric-a-brac of our old church buildings because they smack of the Victorian or Edwardian era, and we make them look like our living rooms—or the ones we see in the ads. This we label change. Meanwhile, many of the fashion setters of this world are going back to Victoria and Edward, and so there is a lively market for old church furniture!

The only change that matters has little to do with all this. It is, as always, something internal. The needed change in worship has to do with how we conceive *ourselves,* not with what we are surrounded by, or whether we kneel, sit, stand, or lie flat on our faces when we pray; whether we drink wine or grape juice; whether we have free or formal prayer. How does the worshiping community envisage itself as it worships? What precisely is it doing and being? More particularly, who is there, in the liturgy, in relation to God, in relation to humanity?

What the Christian community does in its *worship* is the same thing it does in its service in the world. Its worship is an extension of its service, and its service is an extension of its worship. The word *liturgy* (which means "service") should have made that clear.

Worship takes place within the framework of the life of the congregation as *representative* people. When we stand there "before God," we are not just ourselves— this handful of people who made it to worship that morning. We are there in behalf of the others, all the others, representing them before our God. Especially are we there in behalf of the oppressed, those for whom life is not easy, those who have something to quarrel with God about, those who do not readily find the courage to go on: the old ones, the sick and dying ones, the enslaved, the imprisoned, the victims of prejudice, the outcasts of our dominant culture, the political minorities, the poor. Representation does not exclude the dominant, ruling elements of the society (though it is very hard, said Jesus, for the rich); but the priestly identification into which we are called certainly does require a particular solidarity with the victims of the world. We simply have to accept this: our God is like that. He has a penchant for the underlings. And this is not without reason; it is not a mere preference on his part. God knows that in bringing us into solidarity with the poor we will come to a better knowledge both of ourselves and of him. For we are all, finally, poor. "We are beggars," wrote the dying Luther. We are all, finally, dependent upon "sheer grace." The reason why "the rich" have such a hard time entering the Kingdom is that it is so hard for them to know how poor they are.

Identifying ourselves with "the world" and more particularly with those who know that they are poor, and who *are* poor, we come "before God." That is who we are in worship: the representatives. As such we plead the cause of the human race and await the Word of God —or, as it may be, his silence. Our prayers, then, and our hymns and litanies, ought not simply to reflect our own state of being, which may or may not be "comfortable." In solidarity with the world and especially with its victims, we have to be ready to pray and sing some of the more earthy and unlovely things one can hear in the Psalms of Israel. In worship, as in all our life within the *koinōnia* (but especially in worship), we are called to be entirely honest, forthright, open. We too have questions, doubts, deep distrust of the future. Why should these be kept silent? Why should we only tell God how fine he is, and what a wonderful Friend we have in Jesus? "How Great You Are!" "How Good You Are!" No doubt this should also be said—but exclusively? Who would trust a human relationship in which one partner *always* said only nice, sweet things to the other? The root of the unreality of most of our worship lies just here. One feels one must leave outside the door all one's real questions, sorrows, anxieties, criticisms, and fears when one goes into the church. One must only praise, thank, adore, and worship Almighty God! Is there no room for contending with him? Not, I fear, in most conventional Christian churches. There is little of that feverish wrestling with the Ultimate which in reality marks all our lives, openly or secretly. Hence in the great crises of our lives, when what has been secret and hidden comes to the surface—in the dramas of life and death which none escape, few of us feel that "church" is a place that we can go to quarrel with Life. There is a profound weakness in Christianity at just this point, and it is very hard to trace the sources of it. But it is necessary for us to expose our faith to this criticism if we are going to leave behind us, once for all, the unrealities of the Christendom situation and enter the wilderness of the diaspora church. Tackling this question—i.e.: Does Christian faith and theology make any place for the continuing experience of negation?—must become a special part of the whole life of the church that is coming to be, especially its study and its worship.

I have tried to trace the sources of this weakness in my book *Lighten Our Darkness: Toward an Indigenous Theology of the Cross* (Westminster Press, 1976). It is my belief that the weakness in question does not belong to the Christian interpretation of reality as such, but that it is bound up with the great aberration of Christianity which has in fact been the church's dominant stream, and which Martin Luther named *theologia gloriae* (the theology of glory). To this it is necessary to oppose a *theologia crucis* (theology of the cross).

Another significant reason why Christian worship has been so meaningless to a great many people is that it seldom offers anything for the mind. It is divorced from the context of study. Protestants pride themselves on *the sermon* as a great teaching device. They think they have avoided the pitfalls of the liturgical churches by insisting on the importance of the spoken word. This pride is grossly overdone. Especially in the last decades, sermons have degenerated into homilies and pep talks, often of the most childish nature. Indeed, so low has this form of discourse fallen that today "sermon" is almost always a pejorative term. "Don't give me a sermon, please!" Especially is the sermon bound up in most people's minds with morality indoctrination of a certain sort: "Don't preach at me!" In an age of mass communication it is hard for preachers to compete with trained actors and others who can hold the attention of an audience. But besides all that, the church seems to have nothing very special *to say.*

There is no easy cure for all this. But one thing seems obvious: unless worship in general is linked with a continuing life of study on the part of the whole Christian community, preaching in particular will continue to be a hollow undertaking. When the sermon is the distilled wisdom of a trained mind, working together with others over a common aspect of faith and life, a context is established in which it can be heard receptively.

This kind of "participatory preaching" might be realized if the normal worship life of the congregation were to be centered around the house of study. Here the sermon, with all other parts of worship, could grow out of the common life of the community of faith. Since the congregation would be quite small, there is no reason why everyone should not be involved in the preparation and presentation of worship. Not all at once, of course, and not merely as the production of a committee. I believe that it will always be necessary for creative *individuals* to work through the ideas and the art that belong to Christian worship. However, this individual work is normally most creative when it has come out of an ongoing dialogue with others and is meant to speak to issues shared by those to whom it is addressed or in whose presence it is done. With this possibility of sharing, participation, and reflection, the worship of the diaspora church becomes the fruit of its study and the inspiration for its service in the world.

If that is the normal pattern of congregational worship, there should on special occasions—such as the great feast days of the church year—be more impressive *festivals of worship.* On these occasions, the houses of study from a greater area (for example, a larger city, or a group of smaller towns and villages) would gather in one place. A large church building could be kept for this purpose and supported, financially and otherwise, by the houses of study. Why should we not remember what was good from the past and call it a cathedral—or perhaps (recalling our *whole* past) a temple. This one building would be saved from all the others when they had to be sold, torn down, or converted into museums or theaters or whatever. Here, on the festival days, the Christians would come together for celebration. They would hear the best music their musicians could provide; the best art would surround them; those so gifted would enact historic and contemporary drama of the church; the greatest scholars in their midst would interpret the Scriptures and recall them to their worldly vocation. They would be able to experience all this with the hearts and minds of persons who had come to know the tradition of Jerusalem. It would not be a foreign element in their lives, such worship, but a summing up of their study, their communal worship, their life in the world.

The danger that such "triumphant" worship would delude them into believing that the church is still, after all, a "mighty army" would be offset by their daily lives as "little flocks"—the reality of which would be confirmed by their normal form of worship in the synagogue or house of study. In the surroundings of the temple, however, they would be able to feel and to enact something of the mystery and beauty of that greater reality in which their lives and the lives of their little congregations were caught up: the Kingdom. Here in the temple, the individual Christian could be caught up in a reality transcending himself: he would not have to be prominent here; it would be possible to hide, to be anonymous, or simply to *be*—as part of the "body." In the house of study, prominence and active participation would be required of each one, according to her or his ability. Here one could be little, as in relation to the Kingdom of God one really is! Little, but not insignificant. Thus the two sides of worship, being present and being lost, being active and being passive, would be fulfilled.

Is this utopian? Every attempt to envisage the concrete has utopian elements. But it is not utopian if that means indulging in mere fantasy. I have no illusions. There would still be sinners in the liturgical assembly I have described. Insincerity, cynicism, play-acting would still be found there. Some preachers would be pompous, some boring. Some musicians would be prima donnas. Some people would come dressed to impress each other. We are still speaking of human beings. The important thing, however, is not that Christian worship should overcome our humanity but that it should set that humanity in a deeper context. Through it we should be put in touch both with the limitations of our humanity and its grandeur. Worship is for making us real.

The Sacraments

I am not a sacramentalist, if that means someone who feels that observance of the sacraments, especially of the Eucharist, is the essence of the Christian life. There is indeed much that I distrust about sacramentalism as it has been practiced in the church. It has been the means of sustaining questionable priestly (and worldly) power. It has been reduced to sheer magic in the minds of countless Christians (not only medieval Christians!). It has also been a weapon of anti-intellectualism and a symbol of Christian division. Besides all that, in these last centuries it has become a meaningless response to life for many Christians. It appears to keep going mainly on account of the momentum generated by centuries of practice. Most churchgoers don't know why they participate in the sacraments, and a great many participate for what are patently wrong motives.

Yet the two sacraments of Baptism and the Lord's Supper are obviously not arbitrary acts and symbols, with which the church can dispense at a whim. Given a context of understanding and genuine commitment, these sacraments *can* express in perhaps the deepest

ailable to us the nature of Christ's true church.
s as we have identified them include an ongo-
ilentification of the church with the crucified and
risen Lord; the representative character of Christian
existence in the world; and the presence of the Kingdom of God in the midst of this world's kingdoms. It is
not the task of the diaspora church and of those who
prepare its way to dispense with the sacraments recognized throughout our tradition. Rather, it is our task to
recover their meaning.

As a first step in that direction let me raise a critical
question. When are we going to stop making *infant*
Baptism the normative form of Christian Baptism? This
practice, regardless of when it was actually begun, is
based on an assumption that is thoroughly "Constantinian." It assumes that Junior will be a Christian because Senior was. If membership in the diaspora church
is really a matter of individual decision, taken not once
but over and over again (as the Catholic theologian Karl
Rahner has put it), then it is not something that applies
to babies. No amount of theological and exegetical rationalization can overcome that non sequitur.

Let me be quite clear: In claiming that babies and
children should not be the usual subjects of Baptism I
am not saying that they have no place in the Christian
community. That would be absurd. What a sad affair the
koinōnia would be without children—not just on the
periphery, as they in fact tend to be for all our pains at
baptizing them, but at the center! If the basic presuppositions of this book are true, being in God's family is by
no means synonymous with receiving the rite of Baptism. Anyone who still believes that God redeems only
those who are baptized is in no shape to enter the Chris-

tian future. If we are ready to believe that the divine love is expressed in ways far more magnanimous than we can imagine; if we are ready to live in a pluralistic society recognizing that many others with whom we have no doctrinal similarity are nonetheless agents of God's humanizing work in the world; if we are by now ready to entertain the New Testament's own theology of the Kingdom, and not to assume that Kingdom is just another word for church—then surely we are ready to take seriously that our own children are thoroughly within the sphere of the divine love and grace, whether baptized or not.

Whatever arguments have been put forward by Protestant Christians in favor of the baptism of infants, the primary historic motivation behind this practice has been and still is the fear that the unbaptized are not saved. In other words, infant Baptism is a direct consequence of the doctrine *extra ecclesiam nulla salus* (outside the church there is no salvation). This doctrine is of the very essence of that type of triumphalistic Christianity which must be rooted out if Christianity is going to move into the future responsibly and in keeping with its best traditions. Indeed, this doctrine, together with its sacramental and other expressions, has always been troublesome to Protestantism. From the outset it was incompatible with the Protestant critique of ecclesiastical absolutism, as well as with the most characteristic teaching of the Reformation, "justification by grace through faith." As Adolf Harnack long ago pointed out (cf. *Outlines of the History of Dogma,* Book III, Ch. IV, Part IV, pp. 557ff.; tr. by Edwin Knox Mitchell; Beacon Press, 1957), many things that were brought into the Reformation from the Middle Ages, and especially the sacramental presuppositions of the main Reformers, *were* incompatible with the basic thrust of the reforming movement. The error lies not so much with the original Reformers in perpetuating these anachronisms, but with subsequent Protestantism, which ought to have been freer than the Reformers themselves from emotional ties to outmoded practices.

If it is necessary to assure ourselves about the breadth of God's love with respect to our children (and probably it is), then let us devise liturgies of blessing, of thanksgiving, of petition, that can express this. Why not create services for *all* the stages of their young lives; at birth, when they enter the various stages of school and vocational training, when they reach the age of puberty, when they take up this or that challenge in the world? The practice of infant Baptism as a semimagical act has enabled us, apparently, to forget that children are not only born but develop, grow, and mature. Today they mature in a world full of temptations unknown to their parents and grandparents. The shocking neglect of childhood and adolescence in which the Constantinian church has indulged heretofore can no longer be permitted. Our world threatens to destroy the humanity of persons at the very earliest stages of their lives. Infant Baptism and its illogical "follow-up," confirmation, are no substitute for the kind of care and nurture that children need in today's and tomorrow's church.

The reason for questioning the practice of infant Baptism is, in other words, not negative or iconoclastic. It is highly positive and constructive. It asks two things of us: (1) that we do something appropriate and *real* for our children in place of this cultic ritual which is often superficially observed; (2) that we rediscover what *is* significant in the concept of Baptism that can become meaningful for the church of the future and the present. I am convinced that we can only make the latter rediscovery if we cease making *infant* Baptism normative.

We must return to the Biblical tradition of Baptism to rediscover what is significant about it. There we find that it is engaged in by a human being who has lived, who has a past, who has become confused, who has sinned, who has made many beginnings and has failed. Now this human being has experienced a new possibility. Out of the impossibility and jumble of life, a new possibility is offered. Now he or she wants to express publicly, before the congregation and in the presence of God, the fact of this new beginning. "If any one is in Christ, he is a new creature" (II Cor. 5:17).

In short, the most important aspect of Baptism is not the freedom of the person being baptized to will it, to decide. Too often this emphasis conflicts with the Biblical doctrine of grace. It becomes the substitution of "free will" for the sense of being grasped by an irresistible love. I should insist, rather, that the essential thing about Baptism in Biblical thought is the presupposition of *sin.* The person being baptized has a past. This person has tried, has failed, has recognized his or her failure, unlove, and alienation from God and other people. Baptism is the celebration of a new beginning, given in the midst of the life of the "old Adam." It was a travesty of the Christian concept of sin when, in order to fit this Biblical insistence into baptismal theology somehow, Christians began to insist that babies are already sick and damned with sin. That is a totally unwarranted notion, based on an almost complete misappropriation of the Biblical concept of sin. There is no doubt that *the world* into which every new baby comes is sick with sin. No baby, as it matures, will ever be able to avoid the consequences of these "sins of the fathers." Still, to act as if sin were directly applicable to the baby is a travesty of the profound biblical concept of the tragic dimensions of human existence.

I am even prepared to return to the study of the doctrine of "original sin," which liberal Christianity threw out, though (quite inconsistently in this respect) it retained Baptism as the cure for the same. The real meaning of the idea of "original sin" is its insistence that life in this world has a tragic dimension. Life is not just "whatever *you* make it." You were not born into an Eden with all decisions ahead of you. You came into a world already old and sick with human decisions and actions that dehumanized existence. The sins of the fathers are visited upon the children to the third and fourth generations—and then some! Moreover, one does not need infant Baptism to symbolize the priority of God's grace in human life. The baptizing of *sinners* is a far more meaningful and gripping symbol of the prevenience of divine grace than any amount of infant baptizing.

In the future church I envisage, the normal pattern of identifying with the Christian community in a decisive manner would be through a baptism taken in the midst of life. It will express the intervention of a "saving grace," the faith which accepts this intervention and rejoices in it, expressing the courage to engage in a continuing struggle with the dark and damning forces within our being. It would indicate the incorporation into a "fellowship" that can support such courage, and it would indicate the hope of a final identification with the crucified One whose victory over the dark and damning forces within and around us we believe. If Baptism is to become the meaningful liturgical symbol that it potentially is, then *that* is the context of understanding in which it must be practiced.

One further comment on Baptism: I have just said it would be the normal pattern for identifying with the Christian *koinōnia* "in a decisive manner." It has been put quite intentionally in that way because I assume for the church of the future (even more than at present) that there will be many *levels* of association with the *koinōnia*. In addition to infants and children there would be many within the fellowship who are "unbaptized." Some would be "on their way to faith," perhaps; others would be even less committed—some might be agnostic and even atheistic. They would see in this community a place of fellowship, a base of social action, a center for earnest study, and many other things. The church should even seek out such "fellow travelers"— not so much for their sakes as for its own. They would be of enormous help in preventing the diaspora from degenerating into a ghetto, for one thing. From the standpoint of our discussion of Baptism, such persons would help overcome the superstition that Christ's church consists only of the duly baptized. They would help preserve for Baptism a special and truly serious meaning. Instead of treating Baptism as an indiscriminate initiatory rite, it retains for it the power of an act of deeply experienced grace and commitment—in other words, the power of a sacrament.

The vital context of both sacraments in the diaspora church—namely, their occurring in the midst of a small, gathered community—would itself vastly deepen their significance. The baptism of a mature person in the presence of a Christian community whose members know this person, expect that he or she will remain in their midst and contribute in a fuller sense to the corporate life, has a meaning that Baptism simply does not possess in the typical "Christendom" situation. It becomes an act of identification, not only in a personal and mystical sense with the crucified Christ, but in the most public and physical sense with his "body"—these people!

The same context becomes even more important for the Lord's Supper or Eucharist. In the characteristic "Christendom" situation, it is difficult to avoid the connotations of magic in this rite, except where it is turned into a purely "symbolic" gesture. Even in denominations influenced by Zwingli and the left-wing Reformers, the propensity to focus on *the elements themselves* (the bread and wine) in a quasi-magical way is hard to avoid. This is not chiefly because people in such denominations really are open to magic (they aren't!)— although the "medicine of immortality" concept of the sacrament has by no means been confined to Catholicism. It is mainly because the central focus in Zwinglian and other forms of Protestant Christianity should be upon the gathered community in its total act of worship. This consciousness is consistently lacking in the typical Christendom situation of worship. One thinks about the bread and wine in a way that this form of Christianity by no means warrants because there is no real sense of fellowship. One feels like a solitary individual in a group of strangers, although they may be more or less familiar strangers.

In the diaspora situation, it is possible to recover something close to the essence of the Lord's Supper as originally conceived. Here the emphasis is not upon the elements, as if they were in themselves efficacious; it is rather upon the whole being and acting of the congregation "before God." Here the congregation engage in a physical act (eating the same loaf, and drinking the same vintage) through which they reaffirm their identification with the Christ and with one another, and by which they are reconstituted "the body." This awareness of reaffirmation and reconstitution (or renewal) is possible in the diaspora situation as it never was possible in a church that imagined itself the religious dimension of the world at large. In the gathering of the diaspora for this sacrament, there is, to begin with, the consciousness of a *need* to be reconstituted and renewed. Because the constitution of the church is not sustained by social or purely cultural factors, as in the Christendom situation, the diaspora is conscious of a need for its own sacramental reconstitution. Where Christianity is basically indistinguishable from the culture at large, the sacraments generally— and the Eucharist in particular—suffer because *they are not really needed.* I suspect that what many of us experience as the "superfluous" character of the sacraments in typical middle-class congregations has to be put down to this very fact: they are not really needed to hold the congregation together; they do *not* hold it together in fact; it is held together, if at all, by sociological and other factors. Consequently the sacraments (and worship in general) are really not essential. In the diaspora situation, where the sociological props for religion have been removed or cast aside by the church itself, worship in general and the sacramental life of the church in particular become a new kind of *necessity*.

Ministry

What is meant by "ministry" is nothing more nor less than the Christian community ordering its life to facilitate its mission in the world. The form of ministry is determined, in the diaspora situation, by the circumstances of the concrete situation. There is no *one* form of ministry, valid everywhere, in the New Testament's teaching. There is variety. The church was at that point still flexible enough to be able to order its life according to the needs of the moment. Not that it was entirely fluid or without form; but its form served its content—which is what form should always do.

Nor was ministry in the New Testament associated only with individual persons: ministers, priests, bishops, presbyters, deacons. Ministry was and is the task of the whole church. It is understood that individual members must initiate and take responsibility for the various aspects of the work of ministry. We are not dealing here with the *kind* of "group" mentality that one finds here and there in the contemporary church, which thinks that everything has to be the product of a committee! Each one has to make his or her own distinctive contribution. There are different gifts, corresponding to the different jobs needing to be done. Like the various members of the physical body, Paul says, each member of the "body of Christ" has a distinctive and unique function. But this does not give way to individualism, nor does it imply that some are more important than others. Each works as a part of the whole. Ministry is the cooperative work of the whole "body."

From this earlier, shockingly functional concept of ministry, the early church soon developed a highly structured and hierarchical form of ministry. In doing so, the church for the most part simply copied the forms of authority that it found in the world. And it was *authority*, indeed, that governed the whole process of ordering the ministry. The closer the church came to be associated with the official structures of the imperial society, the more its hierarchy reflected these struc tures. In the earliest community, ministry was designed to ensure the better functioning of the people of the cross in their worldly mission. In the subsequent centuries ministry became a way of designating *authority* in church and world.

This tendency of ministry to reflect the structures of authority in society is deeply embedded in the ecclesiastical experience of the centuries. Protestantism often prides itself on having given up the hierarchy of pope and (in many cases) bishops. But it should not be too boastful in reality. The fact is, Protestantism developed under different social structures. Protestantism, after all, was the adopted child of a newly emerging bourgeois civilization. Its orders of ministry reflect, not the feudal society of the older ecclesiastical traditions, but the middle-class structures of the modern world. Our Protestant denominations are still highly conscious of the business and professional world and its system of rank, reward, and authority. Few Christian groups have deviated from this pattern of the centuries. The tendency of the Christians to mimic the world is deep-seated indeed.

The hallmark of the diaspora is its conscious intention to dissociate itself from this tendency. Or, to put it in another way, the diaspora church intends to *disestablish* itself. It no longer feels the need to form itself around the model of the dominant culture in whose midst it lives. It is free to develop its own forms of service, order, and authority—and to let these be determined by what is indigenous to itself, i.e., its gospel and its mission.

An immediate consequence of this is that, wherever it is taken seriously, the whole idea of a "full-time, paid, professional clergy" is being called in question. That does not necessarily mean that such a conventional form of ministry is no longer relevant under any circumstances. It does mean, certainly, that this form of ministry can no longer be regarded as the universal norm. It is perceived, rather, as a historically conditioned form, not as a pattern that inheres in the very structure of reality, not as the essence of the church, not as the unchangeable will of Christ. It may be changed, and drastically changed. It may even come to be the exception rather than the rule. And this may happen far sooner than most church people realize. The question is whether it will happen as an inevitability brought on by economic and other realities, or whether it will happen as a matter of responsible decision on the part of many Christians.

Naturally there is enormous resistance to this analysis. For human and understandable reasons (not always selfish), those who are, like myself, ordained clergy feel threatened by this new situation. We know that the division of the church into clergy and laity is already obsolete. We know that it cannot last, for it is based on an established form of Christianity that is passing away. We nevertheless resist this knowledge, and we avoid forthright reflection on everything connected with it. In particular we resist schemes and alternatives that are put forward by individuals in their own search for more meaningful forms of ministry, or by groups within the churches which try to plan responsibly for the future. We are not ready for the diaspora at this rudimentary level.

Our resistance can be exemplified by citing a concrete instance: A parish minister known to me for many years has for the past ten years of his ministry been working for his living as an elementary school teacher. He continues to be the priest of his congregation. But apart from his rectory and a small travel allowance, he receives no salary from his people.

This man began to prepare for schoolteaching when he had already entered early middle age. He did so at a point in his life and ministry (incidentally, while serving the same congregation where he is still) when he realized that most of the energies of "his" people were employed in raising the money for his salary. He thought that was an unworthy reason for the church to exist. So with the support of the congregation he prepared himself, at considerable pain to himself and his family, to teach school. While he studied, the congregation supported him financially. As soon as he began to earn his modest schoolteacher's salary, this support was withdrawn.

What happened? The congregation itself had to become actively involved in ministry. In the absence of "the professional Christian," everyone had to work. It took time for people to discover their particular gifts for ministry. But some found to their surprise that they could teach classes of children and young people. Others discovered they could lead adult study groups. There was help available—in the form of lay training institutions—for those who took on such responsibilities. More than a few people discovered new reasons for being themselves as they began to engage in ministry to the sick and dying, the organization of social work in the community, the establishment of links with other groups, including other churches, etc. All at once ministry had become the people's business.

The priest in question sees his particular responsibility in two areas: to be the preacher-theologian of the congregation (though not in an exclusivistic sense; mainly because he is theologically trained and an active student of contemporary theology); and to continue to be the liturgist (this being a liturgically-minded denomination), performing whatever ceremonies pertain to this office. Among other things, it is still mandatory that any ceremonies needing state authorization (marriage especially) must be performed by him; and many of the ceremonies to which a post-Christian people still turns to "Christendom" to undertake (burial, for example) become his as well. Incidentally, there is an important need for Christians actively to encourage the development of *alternatives* to Christian or religious ceremonials on the part of the state. It is a mistake to imagine that most people return to "the church" for these occasions because of "residual faith." Often it is simply because such civil ceremonials as are available are so utterly lacking in dignity or meaning. As communist states have demonstrated, civic ceremonials do not *have* to be unaesthetic or perfunctory. Christians should work with others to make such tasteful ceremonials available to people in the pluralistic society that is our context. For one thing, it would help to retain the specifically Christian dimension in marriage, burial, and other rites when they are undertaken in the church.

This example of an alternative form of ministry has been in existence now for almost a decade. It has not worked perfectly. We are still speaking about the church, not the Kingdom of God! But it has transformed the parish. People who were once peripherally associated with the church for traditional reasons, or who were content to sit and watch (as they do in most other situations of life!), or who assumed that the minister should "do it," or who never bothered to ask deeply about their faith—such people have become Christians in earnest, Christian ministers. This one act of a priest who could not justify the form or the manner of his ministry altered the face of a whole parish. How much could be learned from this single experiment!

But for eight years, *no one in the church asked this priest to speak about what has happened.* No one invited him to reflect, publicly, on his experience. No group of ministers, no conference of bishops or governing elders, no theological educators, no young clergy in training—no one, in fact, said to this priest: "Come and tell us about it!" And this is not an isolated instance of neglect.

There are very few such experiments, however, and especially few that have endured long enough to prove themselves. The churches talk a good deal about the need for alternative forms of ministry, for tentmaking ministries, for second vocations for ministers, for experimentation in ministry. We have been speaking about these things for decades. But that is where it stops. The extent of our repression of these approaches as actual, viable alternatives to the "full-time, paid, professional clergy" syndrome is made graphic when someone actually goes out and does something different. In the process an enormous amount of experience is gained, but no one wants to hear about it. Not only that, but it usually happens—as it did in this particular instance—that such experiments in ministry are bitterly opposed. Most of the opposition comes from the church itself, its clergy, its governing authorities. The old system, in which there are obvious but unfathomable vested interests, protects itself with ironclad defenses against such proposals. It can justify itself in the most (apparently) theologically responsible way, with truly sophisticated traditional and Biblical arguments. But it mostly uses rationalization and stalling. It will last, and the form of ministry it justifies will last, only so long as there are dollars to buttress such a luxury. In reality, it has already come to an end, and the malaise of most forms of ministry today can be traced precisely to that fact. The dead are burying the dead.

The diaspora that is coming is necessarily frustrated by this resistance; but it is not utterly discouraged. It knows perfectly well that the resistance will only last as long as there is money to keep it going. In that respect all signs point in the direction of an imminent end. As soon as there are no "pulpits" left for those who want to carry on as ministers in the conventional sense, the present "exceptions" will become more nearly the rule. I am not at all anxious about that transition, though it may well affect my own life. As one who sees at close hand the young and not-so-young women and men who

come to study Christian theology today, I am conscious
of a certain daring and openness in them that even the
best of my generation of theological students did not
possess. We were still the "affable young men" (yes,
mostly men) who could still perceive "the ministry" as
offering us a good chance for personal success and
fulfillment. Our motives were not always questionable,
but they were not so well informed as they should have
been. I am not speaking about the distant past, but
about the 1950's and 1960's. Today there is a greater
awareness, not so much at the intellectual as at the
emotional level, that "the ministry" is something vastly
different from what it has been throughout the centuries. "Becoming a minister" could well mean that after
several years of higher education one would still have
to earn a living in a way unrelated to one's specialized
education. More important, the best of the present crop
of theological students have dispensed with all the ves-
tiges of hierarchical thinking. They do not regard "the
ministry" as offering any special status either in the
world or in the church. In fact, many of them question
the whole concept of ordination for precisely this reason. It is because of them that I *know,* when I write of
a new type of ministry in the diaspora, that I am not
merely engaging in fantasy.

The great responsibility of those who train for special
sorts of ministry will be to *enable* others to minister. The
concept of "enabling" has begun to inform theological
education today, but to date it is far too much regarded
as the development of "skills." Inevitably, the educational world of the churches reflects the educational
world of the society it wants to impress. Therefore the
technical approach to education has taken over much of

what used to be called "practical theology." One studies "pastoral technique" to become a "professional minister." The theological educators have a long way to go before they shall have divorced themselves sufficiently from the establishment to exercise originality and independence in constructing their curricula. What the church needs by way of "specialized ministries" is not merely *skilled* persons but *wise* persons; and there is a vast difference between the two. It is the difference between technique and understanding, between *scientia* and *sapientia,* between know-how and compassion. It is the difference between "the professional" and "the friend," between the sophist and the rabbi. If we could give the little congregations the kind of "enablers" who would help them to understand the gospel and the world, we would be doing more for them than by providing them with people skilled in group dynamics, pastoral visitation, hospital and psychiatric and prison work, etc. In fact, unless the theological educators do provide the occasion for the development of "wise" persons, interpreters of the times and of the tradition, persons who can enable what transpires in the "house of study," this "office" will be filled by others whom the seminaries and theological colleges never see, some of whom may be charismatically inspired, others of whom may be demonically inspired. And the proof of this is that it is already happening in many places!

What is *possible* by way of ministry in the church of the immediate future is so exciting that it makes one impatient with the structures of authority and convention which get in the way of it. On the other hand, the readiness and enthusiasm of many who present themselves for ministry today is a reason to hope that even the established structures of theological education will eventually give way to the possibilities there are. It is therefore not foolish to envisage, in the near future, a diaspora church in which ministry is shared by the whole people of God *(laos),* enabled by persons who are indeed skilled in a variety of things but who are, above all, understanding and who aim more at *wisdom* than at *knowledge.*

I have tried to present a glimpse of the church that is coming to be, could come to be, must come to be. If I can speak about it at all, it is because it is already coming to be—and therefore what I have said in this chapter is in great measure descriptive. I describe what *is*—what I have observed. I have spoken also of what *ought to be.* I have *pre*scribed, not only *de*scribed, because what is coming to be by way of a new expression and model of the church is not yet in a state where one can simply say that it "is," that it exists. It exists here and there; it exists as potential almost everywhere. But it is by no means a *fait accompli,* and there is considerable danger that it will not "come off." For one thing, there is a good deal of resistance to it on the part of the older model and those whose lives are given to its preservation. So it is necessary not only to describe the reality of the new model as it is seen here and there; it is the responsibility of theological observers of this phenomenon today to help to give it birth. They must say why it is right, and why the older model is no longer the right one; they must help to provide substance and courage for the "little flocks" that are taking shape in our midst and that hardly dare to think of themselves as "alternatives" to the great sixteen-century-old phenomenon called Christendom!

One question remains: Is there any way in which this task of the few, of the theologically trained, of the scholars, of the prophets, of the charismatically alive, can be shared by others who, while they are by no means without gifts of their own, feel overwhelmed by the enormousness of the task and humiliated by the church's past to the extent that they cannot consider a future so radically different from it? Or, to put the question much more briefly and crassly: How can we get there?

VII

MAKING THE TRANSITION

An Open Invitation

Our generation of Christians is called to make the transition from "Christendom" to "diaspora." Many of us grasp this intuitively. Some of us consciously attempt to achieve it. We are moved by a sense of urgency, by a feeling of great need.

In some ways this very feeling of need is the reason why we are having trouble making that transition. It is a frame of mind which assumes: This is our job. We have to bring this transition about. The task is enormous— overwhelming! But it is up to us.

It isn't up to us! The church of Jesus Christ is never strictly "up to us." It is *his* church, *his* "body." We have to accept this in the most direct and practical way. So long as we imagine that the future of the church depends upon our insight, ingenuity, planning, and hard work, we will be running on a treadmill. Neither we nor other Christians whom we try to bring along with us will get anywhere. Neither we nor they will be able to believe, in the depths of our beings, that what we are doing has any firmer foundations than our own will and determination.

The church is the gift of divine grace. It is given, not achieved. This does not apply only to the church's beginnings—to Pentecost. It applies to its life all the way along. The *re*forming of the church is as much the work of the Spirit of God as was its initial forming. If we cannot believe that *God himself* is at work in his church, judging its recalcitrance, rejecting the old forms it wants to keep, causing new life to appear where the old dies—if we cannot believe that, then we will not really trust our own reforming activity. Our work of reform is not the initiating work; it is a response to God's initiating work. It is the obedience of faith which wills to participate in the graceful change being brought about by the Spirit.

The transition between Christendom and diaspora, then, is not one that *we* are called to effect. It is a change that is happening. It is God's work in our midst. We are invited to participate in it. This is the first thing we must know about the transition in which we are involved: that it is not ours but God's.

Only if this becomes clear to us will we be able to overcome the sense of heaviness and futility that accompanies so much even of the best reforming activity of Christians today. This heaviness naturally accompanies the prevailing mood of exhortation. Those who feel the need for change most keenly often know no other way to effect it than by exhortation. Concerned pastors address their congregations with urgent appeals for new understanding, a new style of life. Social action groups within denominations assail the churches with brochures that point up the need for intelligent action, gifts, work. Lay and clerical leaders urge greater faithfulness, greater participation, greater support for worthy programs. The effect of all this exhortation is chiefly to increase the sense of futility on the part of both those who exhort and those who hear the exhortations. This is not at all surprising. Under certain circumstances, human beings will respond to exhortation for a time. But behind every "must," "should," and "ought to" there lurks an implicit "Why?" Every wise parent knows about the presence of that silent "Why?" Commands will work only if they are rooted firmly in a framework in which they both make sense and seem possible. If there is any question about the meaning or the possibility of what is urged, the command itself will not suffice. Rather, it will only have the effect of increasing people's cynicism or doubt. *Why* should such changes be made? *How* can they be made?

At issue is really nothing more nor less than the old distinction between gospel and law. Real change is not effected by law. Law by itself can achieve very little. That is why every attempt to reduce Christianity to a morality finally ends in failure. You can tell people to love one another (the Golden Rule!) until you are blue in the face. Unless love is first given, it cannot be shared. "We love, because he first loved us." Before the law of love, there is the gospel of love. Love is the very heart of reality. God *is* love! If I feel this deeply within my life, then I may begin to love. Sensing that I am loved, forgiven, accepted in spite of my unacceptableness, I may then begin to love, forgive, and accept. This is the order of things. Before the commandment there is the announcement. Because "God so loved," therefore you may love. Go: Love! It is possible, so it is necessary. You are permitted to do this, so you are urged, exhorted, and commanded to do this.

In terms of our present discussion, we must understand the great transition from Christendom to diaspora first as something that is "going on" (indicative). It is going on in East Germany, in South America, in the People's Republic of China. It is going on in movements of strange and sometimes questionable character in our own North American world. It is going on within the churches and outside them, sometimes consciously as an explicitly "Christian" occurrence, sometimes far removed from official religious traditions. In countless ways, including ways that none of us can yet perceive or understand, the transformation from Christendom to diaspora is taking place, around us and within us. The question is not whether we will create this new thing, but whether we will participate in it, knowingly and willingly.

It may seem a tautology to make such a point as this. It is simply an axiom of the Christian faith that God takes the initiative in the work of redemption. It belongs especially to the belief of the Reformation churches that the divine grace accounts for everything of ultimate significance (*sola gratia*—by grace alone!). Yet our human pride and slowness of imagination is such that we constantly overlook this axiom. We are tempted again and again to think that it *does* depend on us. And then—since what really needs to be done is *always* far greater than anything we *can* do—we fall into despair and cynicism. If, instead of assailing our fellow Christians with imperatives about the need for change within the church, we began to tell them about the transition that God's Spirit is bringing to pass in our time, we might be surprised at the results.

This study presents the diaspora model of the church

as something "given." It is not an "idea" which I had one day, or which occurred to other theologians and Christian administrators as they brooded on what might be "done." It inheres in the tradition that has been handed over to us from the past; it helps us to make sense of many things that seem to us to be happening to the Christian community in the world today. Thus it is presented, not as a program—a "How To" guidebook —but as a way of naming and understanding what is going on.

This does not mean that the transition from Christendom to diaspora will simply happen whether we accept the invitation to participate in it or not. People have always wanted to distort the meaning of God's grace in that way. If it is God's work, they have said, then let him do it! If it is a matter of "pure grace" and "divine initiative," then surely it will not make any difference whether we affirm it or negate it!

That is of course nonsense. The work that God is doing—in this case we mean his reforming of the church—is not something remote from us, "out there." It is his work with us and within us. When we say that a transition from Christendom to diaspora is being effected by the Spirit of God today, we are saying in the first place that *we ourselves are being changed.* In our own souls and minds, changes are being brought to pass. Some of us can even chart a few of these changes as they have occurred over the years and decades of our lives. We are not the same today as yesterday. Something has happened to us. The expectations that we once had are not the same as the ones we have now. The possibilities we entertain are different possibilities from the ones that we entertained, for example, when we joined the church, or left seminary, or became a member of the official board. We no longer think in terms of success, for example; or we have begun to question the preoccupation of church structures with numbers, influence, power. We have begun to feel more open to movements that we once deeply suspected—Marxist groups, racial, sexual, linguistic, and other liberation fronts. What are the changes that God is effecting *in his church* if not precisely these changes within *us,* individually and corporately?

Do we feel about these changes that we have no part in them ourselves? Do we think of ourselves as simply being acted upon, altered, perhaps transformed, by large and impersonal forces beyond ourselves? Certainly not! There is, to be sure, an element of "necessity" or "destiny" in everything that we experience as *truly* significant. There is the sense that one had to do it. Perhaps even the sense of being driven—or at least of being moved. This is as true of powerful changes in our thinking as it is in other kinds of experience (e.g., love). Yet these changes are not simply imposed upon us. We participate in them. We will them. They come to make sense to us, even though we may feel that the sense they come to make is not of our own devising but something that we discovered. Discovered—not invented.

So to feel that the transition from Christendom to diaspora is God's work does not rob the invitation to participate in it of its meaning. On the contrary, this is what gives it meaning. I can accept the invitation precisely because I can believe that the transforming work in question is grounded in something far deeper and more decisive than my own will. In fact, only as I have the sense of participating in something that transcends both my willing and my very being can I engage in this work of transition with seriousness. Precisely because it does not "depend on me," I can behave responsibly toward it.

Christian Maturity

If the first step is to realize that the transition is not something that *we* are making, the second step would be to appropriate a new appreciation of the meaning of Christian maturity. The vast changes into which Christians are being drawn originate, not with Christian activists, but with the most radical transformer of "the body," Christ himself. To realize this is to be prepared to move to a second dimension of the transformation.

I call this second dimension Christian maturity merely as a convenient way of labeling it. Maturity means many things, of course. It is in fact a rather elusive concept. There is probably very little agreement about its meaning among those who try to define it. But one thing it usually seems to involve is a movement toward essentials. The mature human being is one who has become able to distinguish between what is essential to life and what is unessential. He or she is able to separate the wheat from the chaff, the real from the illusory, the ultimately significant from the trivial or superficial.

Such understanding often entails a gradual simplifying of life. I have known people who have given away most of their possessions. It was not simply an act of generosity; it was because they came to understand their real needs differently. They understood, finally, that they *needed* very little; that they would "be" without "having" very much. The final act of maturity, perhaps, by this logic, would be the recognition that not only "property" but what the world calls "life" itself can be given away. Not thrown away, but given away—laid down for something worthier, for "the friends" for example. "Whoever loses his life will preserve it." It is possible to give even one's *life,* and not to lose what is "essential."

Maturity understood in these terms has at least enough of a relation to the Story at the center of our faith to make one believe that it should have something to say about the character of the church. Theology has always asked about the *esse* (essence) of the church. What would the church have to keep in order to continue to be the church? Would it be the church without buildings? Without any property? Without organs and choirs and pews? Would it still be the church if it did not have a full-time, paid, professional clergy? Would it be the church if it could not count on symbolic or other recognition on the part of the official structures of the society of which it was a part? The traditional "marks of the church" are the ones named in the historic creeds: unity, holiness, catholicity, apostolicity. Would it still be the church if it could not give tangible evidence of these things, even these? Protestantism on the whole said that the "true church" is where the Word of God is faithfully preached and the holy sacraments faithfully administered. This perhaps comes still closer to the "essential." But if there were no pulpits and no preachers in our sixteen-century-old sense, and if there were no Communion vessels or altars or vestments—would the church still "be"? What would it mean for the church to lay down its life for "the friends"? To *lose* its life? What would "maturity" mean for the church of Jesus Christ?

Luther, we remember, said that the only ultimate "mark of the church" is the cross. He meant that the one thing that the church could not give away or give up—the only thing that it absolutely must retain—is its participation in the suffering of its Lord, which is at the same time its participation in the world's suffering. If there is no suffering, no brokenness, there is no church. About the other things he was not so adamant.

This is a provocative thought. And it is not simply poetic! Luther meant it in the most practical way. The most mature church of Jesus Christ would be the one that had finally been able to give away everything, even its life, for something worthier—which we might name "the Kingdom," or the *gloria Dei* (glory of God), or the redemption of the world. For the church too, apparently, it would be possible to lose its very life and retain its "essence." Indeed, we might be moved by many of the words of the Bible to say *find* its "essence." Perhaps the church finds its essence *only* in losing its life!

In any case, there is no doubt that the transition from Christendom to diaspora has to involve loss. The only question is whether we as Christians and churches can experience this loss and gain maturity, or whether we will mourn and lament it—and perhaps be quite debilitated by the whole experience. Will we be able to give away what is unessential, or to have taken away from us things to which we are still deeply attached? I should like to be found on the side of those, in our long "tradition of Jerusalem," who think that very much can be given away without losing what is essential—yes, almost everything.

My intention is to be practical, not poetic. Drawing upon this language of the maturing process, how could we envisage practical steps in the accomplishment of this transition?

Let us imagine a concrete situation: An inner-city church has a prestigious history and a fine old gothic building that in its heyday accommodated nearly two thousand people twice or three times every Sunday. It has a large "plant" besides the sanctuary—"many rooms," as it were. But now the rooms are mostly empty, as is the sanctuary. A few people continue to come. Among them are many old ladies and gentlemen. The few young families find they must bear more and more of the burdens of leadership, financial support, and attendance upon every occasion.

They are not ready to give up. They feel they have something. Perhaps they have something more important than their grandparents had. Their grandparents did all the things they were supposed to do in and for that church because everything around them and within them made that necessary. But these young families, and also some of the older people, are not compelled by anything outside themselves to keep up the institution, to keep the show going. They *could* close up shop, as many of their sister congregations have already done, and as the little white church on the prairies did. But just at this point in their life as a con-gregation—at the point where it all seems to be economically and practically impossible!—they dis-cover the will to be. Perhaps they discover that they *are* something. At the point of their near demise, they reflect upon what they are. It seems precious. This happens to institutions sometimes, as it sometimes happens to individuals facing the limits of their existence.

Someone says to them: "Go out into the highways and byways. There are still people in the apartments round about. You could become a viable congregation if you replenished your ranks with these potential members." But they have tried beating the bushes before, and they know that in the pluralistic society you cannot assume that every apartment dweller is ready to come to church! Not even one in a thousand!

Someone else says: "Amalgamate! There are other churches of this denomination not too far away. Join them. Get together." But they have already amalgamated several times, and they have begun to wonder if the end of this process would mean a final amalgamation into one church building of all the churches in the city, the nation, the world! Is that any way to *face* the problem? they ask.

Various schemes are put forward. Some of them are attempted, halfheartedly. None proves practicable. At last the people have run out of time, money, courage. An impasse has been reached. There is no going back; there is no going ahead either. The pathetic little flock huddles together in services and gatherings everyone knows to be the last. The hymns all sound like dirges now. Meetings are dull and lifeless. The spirit has gone out of the whole enterprise. Once, dreams had been dreamed. Now even the impassioned speeches of one or two of the younger people, appalled by the specter of disintegration, are heard without interest. Everything has been tried before. It seems pathetic for them to remember their earlier enthusiasm—how once they had imagined something might come of this congregation. What is left now is only the burial, the settling of the estate of "the deceased," the mournful dispersion into other congregations that will perhaps, in turn, come to the same dismal end.

A Didactic Interlude

Christians today who confront or can anticipate such a scene as the one I have sketched in the above paragraphs, need to meditate upon two significant parallels in a most serious and practical way.

The first parallel is described in the Hebrew Bible, that earliest and only Bible of the first Christians. It can be read in detail in the book of Exodus. It is about the exodus of a people ("our fathers") from the land of slavery where they were strangely content to a place of freedom they could never quite accept. Moses, that reluctant leader, had finally persuaded them to give up their security, their possessions, and their bondage in Egypt and to wander with God in uncertain places. They believed themselves to be "on the way" to something, and that kept them going, more or less. But they finally found themselves at an impasse: the Red Sea in front of them, and the armies of Egypt behind. They could not go forward; they could not turn back. There was nothing to do but wait for the end, in bitterness and despair.

Then this end became the unlikely locus of a beginning—*the* Beginning, in fact, for the people of Israel still remember it as their primal experience. This Beginning did not appear to them in a magnificent and openly miraculous way, as it has been depicted in popular film and other presentations—amid the wonder of the parting waters! It appeared to them first as sheer impossibility:

The LORD said to Moses, "Why do you cry to me? Tell the people of Israel to go forward."
                                                    (Ex. 14:15)

Forward *into the sea!* Only as they began to go forward did a way open up. But the point is: the way opened only at the point where it seemed ineluctably closed, ended. *Apparently there was something about the nature of the new beginning God intended for them that could only be entered into through the experience of a decisive ending.*

The second parallel to the story I have sketched of the disintegrating inner-city congregation comes from the Bible the early Christians made as they reflected upon their particular experience in the light of the Hebrew Bible. In reality it is the same story. It is always the same story. That is why the Christians came to regard it as their particular foundational story, *their* primal experience. In the most familiar version, it can be read in the continuing account of Luke-Acts.

The little flock is huddled together in a rented room. The rabbi Jesus has been put to death, and they are despondent. No doubt each is remembering his or her own part in the betrayal, and how finally they all left him, their fine protestations of fidelity notwithstanding. But beyond that they know that it is all over now. Whatever they had expected to come of this—this "movement," or whatever it might be—was not going to materialize. Some of them had entertained grandiose plans; but the shepherd had been struck down, and the sheep were about to scatter: back to their old jobs, friends, preoccupations.

Perhaps in a last-ditch effort to prevent everything from falling apart under their very eyes, they began to concern themselves with organizational matters. A business meeting was held, with elections. There should be twelve, and there are only eleven, one having defected. He should be replaced (why?). Perhaps it was the first of that interminable series of boring church meetings which has followed. It was a way of seeming to be alive. But underneath the procedural preoccupations there is the haunting awareness of impending death. Two members of the disciple community, meantime, walking along a road in another part of the region, put the despondency of the whole community into words. "We had hoped that he was the one to redeem Israel," they tell a stranger who has joined them.

Into this heavy, clinging atmosphere there came a breath of real life, like a sweeping wind, a purifying, searing flame. A Presence. Only then! Only at the end —when all their schemes had failed, when human speech no longer inspired, and when dreams had become pathetic memories—then a way opened up, and speech became possible, and memory gave rise to hope.

These two stories differ considerably in detail. But in their basic thrust they are the same. Both affirm that the real Beginning, for the people of God, occurs only through the experience of an ending. Israel began, in earnest, at the point where it seemed to have come to an end. The church was formed at the point where the original expectations of the disciple community had all been brought to nothing.

There is great mystery in this; indeed, it is close to the

central mystery of our faith. But mystery does not mean nonsense or mere irrationality. There is a logic involved in these formative experiences of the people of God—a logic not altogether hidden from ordinary human understanding and experience. We could reflect on the logic of it in the light of a statement made earlier in connection with the description of Israel's primal experience at the Red Sea: Apparently there was something about the nature of the new beginning God intended for them that could be entered into only through the experience of a decisive ending.

There are, after all, beginnings and beginnings. Even in quite ordinary human experience we can discern important distinctions in that connection. It is one thing to start out in the world as a young person, full of youth and vigor, possessed of great expectations and important credentials. It is something else when a man or woman of fifty, having lost a steady job, having experienced personal failure at more than one level, having been humiliated by life, finds the courage to begin again. One does not have to belittle the first beginning, the enthusiastic beginning of youth, in order to find in the second a deeper paradigm of the human condition and a more moving example of human courage. The difference between the two beginnings is more than quantitative—it is a qualitative difference. Between the first beginning and the latter there are not just a number of events which have brought greater knowledge of the world; there are experiences which have brought about an entirely different perspective and which in reality constitute a transformation (sometimes almost a metamorphosis!). The fifty-year-old who has found, somewhere, the courage to begin again is not quite the same person who, twenty or thirty years earlier, stalked into a smart business office downtown to begin a career! Now all the key concepts of human existence have somehow changed for that person. The terms success, failure, happiness, sadness, worth, worthlessness, good, evil, friend, enemy, security, uncertainty, have all taken on a different meaning. Especially has the term "hope" taken on an entirely new meaning. In youth, it meant an attitude of expectancy not difficult to come by, given the general atmosphere of optimism in society. This expectant attitude easily found an internal correlation with a vigorous determination to make good—an attitude one could almost call "natural." Now, at fifty, sifted through the fine sieve of rebuff and failure and despair, hope seems a precious gift, something about which one can never again become presumptuous. It is "hope against hope" (Rom. 4:18).

Maturity is perhaps, at base, precisely that condition in which hope has ceased to be a possession and is seen as a gift: a matter of grace, not of nature.

In the historical language of Christian faith, we are talking about death and resurrection. *The church is the community of the resurrection: that is, it is brought into being, continually, through the experience of dying.* To say that the church is the people of the cross and that it is the community of the resurrection is to say the same thing in different words. As the community of the resurrection it is always being brought to live under the cross. Its "youthful" enthusiasm, its great expectations, its attempts at success, its programs and plans—all that has to be subjected to the cross, i.e., it has to be brought to nothing. This is so, not because God has something against "youthful" enthusiasm and activism (certainly not!), but because he wants us to taste the deeper and truer joys of maturity. To put it another way: God is not opposed to human beginnings. But he is anxious for his creatures to come to that fullest kind of human glory, the glory of "beginning again," beginning after the end. That kind of beginning is what really belongs to us; never to have experienced it would mean to have missed the point and potentiality of our creaturehood —to have remained adolescents. As Elie Wiesel reminds us in his beautiful way:

> According to Jewish tradition, creation did not end with man, it began with him. When He created man, God gave him a secret—and that secret was not how to begin but how to begin again.
> In other words, it is not given to man to begin; that privilege is God's alone. But it is given to man to begin again—and he does so every time he chooses to defy death and side with the living. (Elie Wiesel, *Messengers of God: Biblical Portraits and Legends,* p. 41; tr. by Marion Wiesel; Pocket Books, 1977)

So long as we think ourselves beginners—capable of enormous originality, of creating and mastering our world, of sustaining our own lives—we are adolescents laboring under pathetic illusions. The illusions may be both necessary and acceptable in the teen or twenty-year-old. But a man or woman of fifty who still entertains such illusions is pathetic, as Arthur Miller's "Willy Loman" *(Death of a Salesman)* is pathetic. There is pathos here, not because such a person is offensive in his or her presumption, but because of an inevitable shallowness that external sophistication never hides. Such people are missing a dimension. I have been calling that dimension maturity.

It will be observed that I have moved back and forth, in this discussion, between specifically Christian and generally human experience. In so doing, I am not trying to insinuate that the church is nothing more than a particular form of universal human experience. Obviously what we have to announce as Christians is a quite particular Story—a gospel that points in a unique way to truth that transcends ordinary human experience. At the same time, I believe that this gospel speaks precisely *to* our everyday existence: the existence of persons and societies caught between false hope and despair. The purpose of that gospel is precisely to offer us an alternative, a real alternative to either illusion or death: the alternative of hope, that is, the courage to begin again. The gospel of Jesus announces that we do not have to remain adolescents in our adult years, pathetically posturing as though we were still in our teens when in fact we are already middle-aged (an almost precise symbolic picture of North American society). Nor do we have to fall languishing and jaded into a fatalistic old age, which no longer expects anything of life (the state of many older civilizations in our present world). Rather, we can learn courage at the very edge of peril, expectancy in the face of failure, hope in the dialogue with despair, life as possibility beyond death, resurrection through undergoing the cross. The end is not an impasse. We can begin again at the edge of the Red Sea. We can start afresh after the end of the affair (Pentecost). Beginning again is the only real Beginning, so far as human beings are concerned. And in this time, as—perhaps less dramatically—at all periods in the his-

tory of the church, the church itself is being called to
hear this gospel and to be conformed to the beginning
that appears only at the ending.

The Power of a Suspicion

Let us now return to the congregation that we left at
the point of disillusion—and dissolution! And let us suppose that some members of that congregation (perhaps
only two or three) began just then to entertain something like the thoughts we have been discussing. It
would not be necessary for them to have come upon the
two particular Biblical stories to which we have alluded.
The same story is so much part of the tradition of the
church that it would not be difficult for them to catch
a glimpse of it in one or another form. We can well
imagine that they might begin to see certain parallels
with their own situation.

This, I believe, is where our thought must run in
these times. The first step (a very hard one) is to acknowledge the real ending to which our Constantinian
Christianity has come. Perhaps we can still expect only
a minority of churchgoers to get this far. Once this step
has been taken, the next one is not as difficult. It involves the growing suspicion that this decimation of the
church, this humiliation of Christendom, this "judgment beginning at the household of God" may after all
contain a certain logic; the beginning we are meant to
envisage could only be possible through the experience
of an ending. Without these two primary steps—the
perception of the end, and the suspicion of a beginning
in it—I am convinced that all church deliberation and
planning today is vain. Apart from such a perspective

the future of the church for which we plan only turns out to be another version of the old Constantinian model.

Let us not underestimate the power of that "suspicion" with which the second step begins. Those who have not been able to acknowledge the end of Christendom are often prevented from doing so because they have not been able to sense anything of the new beginning that is already in it. Hence they imagine that the only alternative to bolstering waning Christendom would be complete capitulation. That is far from the case. The sense of a beginning-in-the-ending is not merely a romantic concept. Indeed it can be the most exhilarating of all human experiences. It translates itself into every moment of depth in our personal lives: the experience of finding love after alienation, friendship after enmity, home after the strange land, companionship after loneliness, forgiveness after guilt, meaning after exposure to the purposelessness of the age, health after sickness. In every case, the positive element (new beginning) is made more poignant and compelling by the negative experience. It is the end which gives the beginning its quality, its joy.

The parables of Jesus almost always contain this insight. They have power because they touch upon this very human experience, this suspicion that the very thing which negates somehow *serves* the good. The prodigal returning to his home finds it more truly *home* than it could have been if he had never gone away. There is joy in heaven (in heaven!) over one sheep that was lost and found. A merchant is ecstatic upon discovering one really precious jewel, the worth of which he could not have recognized had he not spent so much of

his life accumulating inferior gems. A housewife rejoices with her neighbors upon finding her lost coin. A
persistent old lady is finally "vindicated" by a judge who
for a long time has refused to listen to her case. By this
same token the primary vocation of Jesus in the New
Testament is that of a healer of spiritual/physical dis-
ease. He himself is reported to have commented that
only the sick need a physician. Only those who have
experienced the real limits of their creaturehood can
know the grace of unexpected extensions—of beginning again. It may be that there is no more potent and
transforming spirit abroad in the life of humanity than
that spirit which leads them through endings into new
beginnings.

There is of course an antithetical spirit which is almost as powerful. It is the spirit which tempts us to give
ourselves over to the endings, to death, to oblivion.
Freud, among others, has charted the movements of
this demonic spirit. It should not be overlooked by anyone who sets out to discuss the present state of the
church. Many church members today would rather *seek
an end* than submit to the anxiety of awaiting it. The
"death wish" applies to institutions as much as to individuals. It would not be surprising, then, to find in
many congregations persons whose activity (and inac-
tivity!) was informed by the hidden or open assumption
that capitulation was the inevitable end of the process.
There can even be a kind of sick satisfaction in nurtur-
ing such an attitude.

Is not the secret of this "death wish" the fear that
death is the last word? We *wish* for death because we
do not enjoy *waiting* for it. We are led to *seek* the end
in order to shorten the time of our anxiety about its

imminence. We want to be decisive! To do something! Not passively to await the inevitable, but to anticipate it—jump the gun on fate, close the doors before they are closed. This is indeed a powerful spirit, especially in the modern world, for it is born of the modern determination to master. But what if "the inevitable" is challenged by that other spirit? What if the suspicion grows that the doors which are closing are being closed for some good reason? Perhaps they are not being closed by an impersonal destiny but by a providential God who wills that his church should find again that one, narrow door, before entering which—if one is to enter—one must be brought very low? What if the suspicion appears here and there in old, dying Christendom, that its end contains a new and authentic beginning?

That suspicion, when it begins to take hold of a congregation—or even of only "two or three" within it—is no mean thing. It is not to be written off as a mere whistling in the dark, or a new bid for success, or another bright design for church "renewal." Where it is genuine, it will want to distinguish itself sharply from mere "bourgeois optimism," success orientation, and the revitalization of ecclesiastical strength. It will be differentiated from all that in particular by its attitude toward the end of Christendom. In the first place it will not be afraid to face that end squarely and openly. In the second place it will regard that end in an attitude of sober joy. Without being flippant or superior, it will welcome that end. It will see the end of Christendom as the necessary accompaniment and presupposition of a renewal that is real. We should not mistake it: the death of Christendom, the decimation of congregations, the falling away of many, the loss of ecclesiastical power and glory, the reduction to a minority—*all this can really be received today, by faith, in a mood of joy and expectancy.* This will be, not the joy of the nihilists who love to push over what is falling, but the joy of the Christians who assess all of this according to the paradigm of death and resurrection. Such joy and expectancy is not therefore the prerogative of a few—an elite, the theologically sophisticated. It can be experienced by anyone who takes seriously the Biblical model of the people of God. Once the vision of a beginning-in-the-ending is introduced into the life of a congregation, there is no telling where it will lead.

Let us imagine, then, that such a powerful suspicion began to inform a few among the members of that dwindling city congregation. What might happen? Concretely and explicitly speaking, "there is no telling." But in terms of broad, rudimentary developments within the life of such a congregation, we might, I think, reasonably speculate on *four probabilities.*

1. *They would stop feeling ashamed of being little.* This at first may sound negative, but, given the facts of ecclesiastical existence, it is highly positive. The church is so consistently dominated by majority consciousness, success orientation, and the quest for power, that the sheer fact of growing smaller is enough to debilitate most congregations. It can be demonstrated convincingly that when groups exceed one hundred persons the kind of community the Christian church has always said it wants to foster becomes impossible. By that standard, most of the churches on this continent—being made up of less than one hundred persons—are numerically speaking "just right." But we are so overwhelmed by growth expectations that we are incapa-

ble, for the most part, of exploring this advantage. Until we are prepared to "think little," we shall simply melt away in embarrassment over our actual littleness. The primary development within our hypothetical downtown congregation would be that wondrous discovery that it is perfectly all right—and indeed "just right"—to be a "*little* flock." It has to begin there. Without that beginning, there can be no real resistance against the prevailing aim of making the congregation big (big again, usually) in order to make it acceptable and "viable." What must take shape among us is the courage to fight this mentality—in others and in ourselves—with the theological and even sociological insistence that in reality the only truly viable *Christian* congregation is a small one! This is what we implied when we spoke about "beginning where we are."

2. *They would consciously begin to seek their true essence.* The first step is polemical. We have to fight off the remnants of a powerful, destructive image of the church in order to take seriously the reality of the existing congregation. The second step is constructive. When we discover that the church wasn't intended to be what we had been led all along to think it ought to be, we are in an excellent position to learn what it *is.* This we learn from our sources, from elements of our long history which have been neglected or distorted, from other churches in the world today (particularly in the Second and Third Worlds) that have had to rethink their reason for being. The search for the true essence of the church is the most exciting task that has come to us in this generation. The re-searching of our past, the study of Scripture, and exposure to the questions of the world—when born of the genuine, existential *need to*

know—can be an undertaking unlike anything the churches of this continent have ever experienced. Such a study has little in common with what has been called "Christian Education." While the pursuits of the latter were never without potential for transcending themselves, they have rarely achieved that transcendence because they were undertaken in the Constantinian situation—that is to say, under conditions where this research, study, and wrestling with the content of the faith was only secondary, since the continuation of the church in the world was apparently guaranteed by other factors. At the end of the Constantinian era we know that without the most rigorous search for understanding of what is believed, belief is doomed.

All great transitions and revolutions, whether at the personal or the political-social level, begin with a renewed exposure in depth to "the ontological question": Who *am* I? What *are* we? It always implies something painful, because it is painful to have lost the old, assumed "answers" to such questions. But it is also exciting—the very stuff out of which life is made. It is the frank recognition that our being is greater, more mysterious, and more elusive than our attempts to define it. New wine needs new wineskins. The search for the "essence" of the church of Jesus Christ will become the primary intellectual and spiritual search of the congregation that begins to be grasped by the sense of a beginning in the end.

3. *They would begin to discover God's world.* Again and again concerned individuals within and outside the churches ask in bewilderment or anger why the Christians have so little knowledge of, or involvement in, the world. The reason is complex in terms of specifics. The

Christian church long ago worked out its basic arrangement *vis-à-vis* the world, and—except for upsets here and nuances there—it has not until now, in the Western world at least, had occasion seriously to doubt these working arrangements. We have explored, in Chapter VI, the relationship between church and state, the church and various movements and causes, the church and other religions. So long as the congregation is enthralled by this understanding of itself in relation to society, it is insulated from any original form of encounter with "the world." Its relation to society and all of its institutions, classes, and groups is already defined and circumscribed by the working arrangement in question. The World Council of Churches is experiencing considerable criticism from segments of the church because of its support of certain liberation movements within the Third World context. Criticism arises because the council has sought to aid a dimension of the world that is not included within the terms of this working arrangement. In other words, under the conditions of "establishment"—in whatever form it may have been conceived—both "church" and "world" are carefully delineated and their essences well known.

But when the church begins to know that it does not know itself, its own essence, it also realizes that it no longer quite knows what the "world" is. After all, the "world" is never something singular or simple. Now there are several worlds. We speak of the Third World. There is also a First and a Second World. Suddenly many Christians find themselves confronted with this plurality of the world. They begin to realize the ways in which they have aligned themselves with one "world" *against* the others. They have done this as individuals who by birth and citizenship belonged to one of the three "worlds." They have done this also as Christians, who claimed the universality of the divine love and of human brotherhood.

The congregation that begins to search for its own true essence cannot go far along that path until it meets a "world" that it does not know. It cannot categorize that world in advance. It cannot "relate" to it in the conventional ways. What will come of this meeting one cannot predict. It is full of possibilities. Perhaps no other aspect of what may happen to the church that faces its end/beginning honestly is so fraught with possibility as this—the church's new discovery of God's world.

4. *They would begin to simplify their life.* I am referring to what was said earlier about "becoming mature." To begin to discover the essence of the church is at the same time to begin to discover the unessential. The accidental things, the things that have been picked up along the way, seem now to have little or nothing to do with our actually *being* the church in the world. Most of what was necessary to the church established here on earth is completely unnecessary in the diaspora situation. Not only is it unnecessary; most of it is a detriment. No rules can be laid down that will apply in every situation. It would follow from most of what has been said that on the whole "church property" is a category that must increasingly be designated unessential, often detrimental. The stipends of ministers, organists, and other employees of churches will also have to be called more and more seriously into question. Here, however, I am not chiefly interested in the particulars of what is retained and what is given up in this or that situation; what interests me is the process itself. In one form or

another, the congregation of our inner-city church would undertake this sorting out.

And it would engage in this task in a mood, not of mourning and dejection, but of discovery and celebration. I picture a congregation that would set for itself a kind of ultimate goal, with stages along the way. A five-year plan, it may be! The goal would be some external and symbolic manifestation of a new maturing. Along the way, at set stages, the unessential things would be let go of. Why stages? Because there are practical questions to be considered, such as the welfare of persons who may have depended for their livelihood on church stipends and the disposal of properties. Also because it would be possible only in this way to bring many persons in the congregation into the process of elimination and discovery. Letting the unessential go can only be a matter of deliberate celebration if a congregation really believes that particular aspect of its life to be less than "of the essence." It must have grasped something of what the "essence" is, definitely and concretely, in order to have the courage to say that this or that (which may indeed have seemed the quintessence of the church for centuries!) is no longer needed.

The task of letting the unessential go is a difficult one. *But it can be done.* The needed courage can be discovered. Moreover, it can be evoked from persons in the churches today whom most of us might consider resistant to change. For example, it is often said that "the old people" will object, or "conservative clergy" will squelch the idea, or "the men" or "the women" will stand in the way. Without meaning to minimize the reality of resistance, we must be critical of all such classifications. Surely, in a church that almost universally recognizes its growing plight in the world, there is a greater openness to experimentation in all quarters than many would-be reformers are willing to admit. At the very least, no group or element within the church should be written off in advance as being incapable of entertaining truth!

CONCLUSION

There are really two conclusions, for two different sets of readers.

In its title, this book states a question that for many Christians seems impertinent; to some it will even appear irreverent. For these persons, if they have read the foregoing pages, I would simply express the hope that now they at least understand why such a question might be asked, and that it could be asked in a reverent way. Beyond that, I hope they have been brought to wonder whether the future of the church may not, by God's grace, be very different from the future it has always *wanted* to have.

For the other set of readers—the one in fifty for whom the future of the church *is* a serious question, with no obvious answer—I have a different concluding word. What I have wanted them to hear is that it is possible and proper to ask this question openly and in great earnestness, facing squarely its negative dimensions, and still to end with a Yes that is not just "cheap hope."

To these I offer a concluding confession. I will just whisper this: To my surprise I find myself more hopeful today for the future of the church of Jesus Christ than

I have ever been in my lifetime. I have hope in the Biblical sense of the word: hope not as a matter of sight, but of faith. Early in my life as a Christian, under the influence of a kind of theological certitude, I had no occasion to doubt the future of the church. It was assured. Not even the gates of hell could prevail against it. But this attitude was not produced by hope; it was the product of a theological ideology, a matter of fact! Later, having been swept rather clean of that particular assumption, I found myself turning toward the opposite extreme. Nothing so insipid, so devoid of discipline and excellence, so indistinguishable from the social wallpaper as the churches could expect any sort of future.

Changes have occurred—both in the churches and in me. The last remnants of a former affluence have almost departed from the churches previously styling themselves "major denominations." With this economic and numerical diminution some of their former bravado has also left them. The element of "unreality" still clings to much of ecclesiastical life, especially in its more official manifestations. It is not possible to become complacent in our hope for the churches. There are enormous dangers still on every side. But there is also a new openness to radical change, especially in the churches most seriously affected by the inroads of secularism, pluralism, and hedonistic apathy. There is also a new dissatisfaction with *superficial* change. It is as if, at the point of her historical demise, old lady Christendom here and there becomes capable of great clarity and honesty.

It is just at this point, then, that those who care about gospel, church, and world, and who are competent to provide resources of understanding and courage, should be rallied to the support of "the old Lady." Too many of the most articulate and concerned disciples of Jesus Christ have left the churches, either in the body or in the spirit! Some still associate themselves with this or that congregation, but without enthusiasm or expectation. This flight from the empirical church is understandable. It has always been hard to take the gospel seriously and remain within the church visible. But the flight of so many of its most gifted sons and daughters has meant the increasing prominence, within the church, of its more mediocre and superficial elements. If in these "last days" the churches are confused and baffled over what is happening to them, it may be because they lack the leadership of persons capable of understanding the tradition, the gospel, and the present circumstances of the world.

I believe that a future presents itself to the church today. It seems to me to be a future consistent with what is *best* in the church's past. But this future is *possible*, not *inevitable*. Its possibility is a matter of grace: God is offering, in new and historically unprecedented ways, to create out of the ruins of Christendom a witnessing community that is truly salt, yeast, seed, and light. As always, it is a creation out of nothing. Whether it amounts to anything will depend in great measure on whether this offer is taken up by Christians who can match its boldness with understanding, faith, and the courage to "begin again."